HAUNTED
JEROME

HAUNTED JEROME

PATRICIA JACOBSON AND MIDGE STEUBER

Haunted America

Published by Haunted America
A Division of The History Press
Charleston, SC
www.historypress.com

Cover image: The ruins of La Victoria Market, also located in the bordello area. *Copyright Ron Chilston.*

First published 2019

Manufactured in the United States

ISBN 9781467141659

Library of Congress Control Number: 2019939724

Notice: The information in this book is true and complete to the best of our knowledge. It is offered without guarantee on the part of the authors or The History Press. The authors and The History Press disclaim all liability in connection with the use of this book.

I would like to dedicate this book to my parents, Irvin and Sara, and my siblings, Karen and Jimmy, for their love and encouragement. Although my parents and brother are no longer with us, my family's inspiration and support are forever present in my life.

–Patricia S. Jacobson

To all who work for truth and justice and aspire to live as kindly and compassionately as possible.

And for the ghosts—may they be heard.

—Midge Steuber

CONTENTS

ACKNOWLEDGEMENTS

With much gratitude and appreciation for the artists who have shared their skills with this project: Michael Thompson of michaelthompsonphotographer.com, Ron Chilston of jeromephotos.com, Steve Mullensky of Quality-of-Light Photos, Cody DeLong of Cody DeLong Studio and Jason S. Voss of Tours of Jerome.

Thanks also to our own Jerome Historical Society and its board of directors for granting permission to publish a selection of archival Jerome photographs. Please note that the addition of the Jerome Historical Society photographs does not mean that they are endorsing the ghost stories—please see the disclaimer.

Unbounded gratitude for Jerome's own Rosa Cays, for her heart and editing skills in taking the words of these two rowdy authors, cleaning them up and giving this manuscript a sense of flow. Yeah, Rosa!

A special thanks to the helpful staff of the Sharlot Hall Museum Library and Archives Research Center, who were always eager to help us.

Sincere gratitude to our friends and community members who have shared their experiences with us. We wish to thank the following for their contributions to this book (last names are omitted intentionally): Lonnie, Renee, Bill, Manuela, Steve, Terri, Ron, Ruth, Tony, Vanessa, Pamela, Ron, Leigh, Mary, Anne, Julianne, Peggy, Sally, Andrea, Roberto, Joshua, Larry, Scottie, Cindy, Pat, Carlos, Chuck, Nicole, Jane, Jackie, Jason, Ron, Andrea, Melissa, Kim, Ellen, Leigh, Debra, Deborah, Andrea and Jessica. We can imagine that it's possible that one or two names may have been unintentionally omitted and would like to apologize in advance for any errors or omissions.

I also must express my sincere gratitude and appreciation for my coauthor and researcher extraordinaire, Patricia Jacobson. Her passion for Jerome and its history goes way beyond what words can describe. Thank you, my good friend; I would not have taken on this project without you.

A huge shout-out to some strong women friends, Patricia Patterson and Cindy Espolt, both of whom held my hand, encouraged me and helped in numerous ways with this project.

Another huge shout-out of gratitude to Terri Straley, Julianne Shuff, David Hall and Jane Moore, all of whom helped in many ways.

Lastly, we want to thank the ghosts, spirits and entities (you choose which name you like), without whom this book wouldn't exist.

With love to our friends and families of choice and origin.

For further information and additional photographs of Jerome, you can seek out the companion book on Jerome in the Images of America series by Arcadia Publishing.

INTRODUCTION

Welcome to the mother lode of all Arizona ghost stories. Jerome, Arizona, holds the distinct title of being the largest ghost town in America, as well as the country's first "ghost city." It is said that Jerome is home to more spirits than earthlings.

Jerome became a ghost town soon after the mines closed in the early 1950s, when the population dwindled to fewer than one hundred people from a peak population of more than fifteen thousand. Many of the remaining Jeromites were elderly and from large families. Some of those who owned grocery stores ended up with several houses when the last of the residents gave their house keys to the grocers as they left. It was how they repaid them for having seen them through with food during their last days in town.

The story of Jerome is one of strong, creative and spirited people. Its collective character can be summed up in both the past and the present as a fiercely independent community that is outspoken, marches to a different drummer and holds a can-do, never-say-die attitude.

Jerome's original pioneer history began with a billion-dollar copper mining camp, a fast-growing, wild and rambunctious boomtown that became the second-largest city in Arizona at the beginning of the 1900s. With all its prosperity and rowdiness came opium, drinking, prostitution, gambling and violence. The *New York Sun* declared Jerome the "wickedest town in the West" in 1903.

Jerome also became the largest city in northern Arizona, possessing all the amenities. There was a Masonic temple in the T.F. Miller Building, two brokerage houses selling shares of mining stock, two opera houses, three

Main Street before all the wooden buildings were burned down. The Grandview was replaced by the Bartlett Hotel. *Courtesy Jerome Historical Society.*

Lives were instantly lost and the Marion 300 destroyed in 1926 when it hit an unexploded coyote hole. *Courtesy Jerome Historical Society.*

bowling alleys, gambling halls, more than eighty-six saloons from 1900 to 1916 and many "ladies of the night." One famous prostitute happened to share the author's name of Midge, or Midgie, as she was known. She was a "soiled dove" who worked for Belgian Jennie Bauters. When Midgie was busy, Jennie would give the waiting men more whiskey until Midgie could accommodate them. Ah, just another example of Jerome's exceptional hospitality and sense of looking after one another!

An article in the *Camp Verde Bugle* in 2003 noted that "the underpinning of all of the history, of all the lives that collectively make up Jerome, was the ore, the lure of extracting enormous wealth from hard-rock mineral. Without the ore, there would be no Jerome." When copper prices dropped and the ore body played out, the copper mining company closed the last mine in 1952.

During its heyday, people in Jerome succumbed to mining accidents and gunfights, overdosed on opium and suffered many other unnatural events. Many of Jerome's "sporting ladies" met disastrous ends by way of murder. With its hard-earned past, it comes as no surprise that Jerome is filled with wandering spirits. However, there was blood on the land here before the

Artist rendering, oil: *38 Fat Tire Ford*. A fitting image for Jerome when folks began leaving. *Copyright Cody DeLong*

mining days. Native Americans and Spanish conquistadors had already discovered the rich earth of Jerome's mountaintop locale. Although most of the stories shared here appear to date from the mining history, a few do involve Native Americans.

According to the Jerome Historical Society, in 1953, speculation ran high that the entire town of Jerome would be razed. A former official of Phelps Dodge Corporation said, "Within a year, grass will grow on the main street of Jerome—Jerome is finished."

To save Jerome and bring in tourism, a historical society member dreamed up a sign that cemented Jerome's reputation. It dramatized the town's dwindling population in a sequence of descending numbers, each with a line crossed through it: ~~15,000~~, ~~10,000~~, ~~5,000~~, ~~1,000~~…. At the end of the sequence were the words "GHOST CITY." Press releases followed, and soon Jerome became known as "America's First Ghost City."

Things in the ghost town were strange, so much so that people from surrounding areas would come up to Jerome to go through the empty and deserted houses. Some of the homes still looked inhabited, as if the family had just gone out for ice cream. The rooms were furnished, dishes were stacked in the cabinets and clothes hung in the closet. It became a source of entertainment to see what could be found in these abandoned homes. Needless to say, vandalism followed. Nobody ever thought people would

Ghost City sign and view of Jerome photographed from the Hogback. *Courtesy Jerome Historical Society.*

want to live in Jerome again. As a result, many of the old buildings were sold for salvage and taken down.

Unbeknownst to the historical society, while all this was happening, the ghosts of Jerome were already very active. Jerome holds a rich tapestry of undeniable ghosts and hauntings, many of which are similar sightings repeatedly recounted by total strangers.

It's no wonder we have several local businesses with ghost or spirit names: Spook Hall, Haunted Hamburger, Ghost City Inn, the Spirit Room and the *Ghost Post*, a former town newsletter.

Flatiron Building at the intersection of Main and Hull. Note the large stone roadway prior to paving. A rough historic neighborhood. *Courtesy Jerome Historical Society.*

Jerome's hauntings, ghost sightings and paranormal activities happen throughout the town and geographic area, in various buildings, streets and outdoor locations. After a chapter on the history of death in Jerome (ghosts come from somewhere, right?), our stories begin with the building that has been described as the most haunted in all of Arizona: the Jerome Grand Hotel. It was the town's fourth hospital, built by the United Verde company to care mostly for sick and injured miners. Two other medical facilities existed—and were needed. One was in the old Jerome High School building, and the second was in the Little Daisy Hotel.

In 1967, Jerome was designated a National Historic District by the federal government and a National Historic Landmark in 1976. Today, Jerome is a significant tourist destination, with most of the existing old buildings restored and repurposed.

To give you a sense of the feeling here in Jerome today, I will quote you something from my first Jerome book. I had asked several locals if they had one word or phrase that best describes Jerome for them. The first response was "a sense of community." Another response from a past Jerome mayor, Jay Kinsella, was "blessed." And lastly, from longtime resident and owner of Paul and Jerry's Saloon, the late Jerry Vojnic: "family."

Jerome people look after one another. We have a community Christmas potluck dinner party as well as a children's Christmas party, Santa included, for families who live or work in Jerome. These Jerome Christmas parties originated back in the time of Rawhide Jimmy Douglas, whose former mansion is now the Jerome State Historic Park.

Halloween is Jerome's favorite holiday, celebrated in every possible way. This includes a not-to-be-missed masquerade ball hosted by the Jerome Volunteer Fire Department at Spook Hall. The forty-fourth annual fundraiser will take place this year in 2019! Jerome sits on one square mile of land, yet the service area of the volunteer fire department is two hundred miles.

Visitors come from all over the country on Spook Weekend near the end of October for the annual homecoming of hundreds of former Jeromites, who return to their town to share fellowship and memories. These strong homecoming turnouts repeatedly demonstrate the great love and magnetic pull that Jerome has on its residents, past and present. We hope this book will give the Jerome visitor a strong visual sense of its historical past, as well as the enchanting magic of the community.

One of our longtime residents, a rare one who actually grew up in Jerome, described what it was like:

Photograph taken in 1910. Standing in this location today, you can still see the Connor Hotel and Fashion Saloon. *Courtesy Jerome Historical Society.*

I lived in my house up on Magnolia, and the door would always fly open, even when it was not windy. The silverware would jingle in its drawer. I could even hear it when I was in the shower. Growing up here, I always knew that there were spirits. Since I was a kid hanging out in the park, I would see weird people that were dressed unusually, and I didn't know why. It's as though time isn't so linear here. Maybe it's all happening at the same time. It became the norm. You know, it wasn't like "Oh, there's a weird guy," or "Oh, I felt a cold breeze," or "Hey, the door flew open—check and make sure nobody is out there. Oh, nobody is out there. OK, close the door." It was just part of life.

Hold on to your seat, your hat or your pants and enjoy.

DISCLAIMER

With a subject matter like this, you can imagine that it would be next to impossible for us to verify the stories we hear. And it may even be tempting for people to make up stories with the hopes that theirs may be chosen for publication.

INTRODUCTION

When I first moved here, I was told by one of my neighbors that one reason he enjoyed meeting town visitors was because he could say anything about Jerome and they'd believe it. Unfortunately, I have heard this still happens today. We have chosen to share only legitimate stories where the person interviewed sincerely believed they had experienced a real spirit. We want to assure you that we have decided to include stories only from those we know with credibility. Patricia has lived in Jerome for thirty-nine years, and I have been here for sixteen years.

What we have here is a group of residents and visitors from all walks of life. Some people are open and eager to share their stories. Others choose to be anonymous for various reasons. Other ghost sightings and reports come from research we have done, and many are repeated sightings seen by several different people.

The point we want to make here is that we have made considerable efforts to report only actual sightings—no made-up marketing ploys. Despite these efforts, we really have no real clue that any word of this is in fact true.

The spirit experiences we have written about came mostly from interviews conducted in 2018. Given more time, we're sure we could publish a series of books on Jerome ghosts alone. Our greatest challenge has been choosing which spirit encounters to include in this book. As mentioned in their respective chapters, the Jerome Grand Hotel, Ghost City Inn and Connor Hotel all keep journals of their guests' spirit experiences, and they fill several volumes each year!

When known, we share the history of the location where the haunting occurs so you may understand why this particular spirit may still reside here in Jerome. As she works hard to research and discover each haunting, Patricia is always asking herself a question: "What happened at this location in the past? Who might these spirits be?"

I began this book project as a complete skeptic on the existence of ghosts—I have done a 180 on my beliefs now. There is definitely something paranormal going on here in Jerome. The sincere and passionate stories I have heard have opened my mind and turned my head completely.

It is with a humble spirit that we offer this book on haunted Jerome for your enjoyment.

Regarding photographs from the Jerome Historical Society Collection, note that the archival photographs acquired from the society are not to be construed as validation or authentication of any of the enclosed "ghost stories."

"BOO HA HA"

WHAT COULD HAPPEN?

WHO ARE ALL THESE SPIRITS?

This rugged mining camp high on Cleopatra Hill worked hard and played hard. Jerome grew fast and furious, and with growth came natural disasters, horrific mining accidents, many fires, flu epidemics and several homicides, all of which account for numerous deaths and potential spirits.

Roberto Rabago stated in his book, *Rich Town Poor Town*:

> *Jerome has been providing ghosts ever since the mines became big business, and that happened very early....It is the energy of the emotions of those who die frustrated, helpless, and angry that creates a ghost....That is why there are so many, especially around the hospitals, where many of them spent their last days in the world, alone, helpless, wanting help and not getting it.*

A brief review of Jerome death certificates finds numerous fatal mining accidents from falling down mine shafts, having limbs blown off or burned off, skulls smashed by boulders, accidental electrocution, cave-ins, carbon monoxide poisoning and more. You can imagine how incredibly dangerous it was to work in the mine.

Jerome was also seriously troubled by landslides caused by the extreme blasting in the mines. Amazingly, they would dig tunnels and pack them with explosives ranging from 50,000 to 200,000 pounds. Massive landslides would then, in turn, cause extensive damage throughout Jerome.

An example of a horrific mine blast was described by Herbert Young in *They Came to Jerome: The Billion Dollar Copper Camp*, in which he stated, "The Grand Daddy of all mine blasts was exploded in a tunnel 110 feet long....The explosive charge was 260,000 lbs, the equivalent of six standard freight carloads. Windows rattled all the way to Camp Verde!" What he didn't mention is that half the businesses on Main Street were destroyed from this blast.

Homicide was a common occurrence in old Jerome. Further scanning of death certificates indicates that many were killed by a gunshot wound to the head, gunshot wound to the neck, gunshot wound to the stomach, being stabbed with a knife, strangulation, accidentally shot in the back and more. Not only were the mines not safe to work in, but the town was a dangerous place to live as well. You begin to understand how Jerome earned the title as the "Wickedest Town in the West."

The miners of the 1880s and early 1890s were brave men, and until they got protective gear, they went into the mines without helmets, carrying a lunchbox, a canteen and a candle. There was no protection for their heads, and their candles would ignite gases and flammable particles. That is why the accidents were so horrific. The miners were paid about three dollars per day, and there were no limits to the lengths of their shifts, usually twelve hours. It's ironic, then, that U.S. Senator William Andrews Clark, owner of the United Verde Mine, was in on the vote that made the eight-hour workday into law.

Four Jerome lawmen were killed in the line of duty from 1891 to 1933. Constable James G. Hawkins was killed by prisoner Tom Gallagher on April 19, 1891. Officer Charles Emmerson King was killed on August 27, 1910, when he was shot in the back by a drunk. Deputy Sheriff James Lowry was shot to death in an attempt to break up a fight on July 16, 1918. Lastly, Officer Dave Rees was found dead at the Nevada Café on May 22, 1933, shot in the stomach. The culprit was never identified.

Pat relayed the story of a murder in Otto's Place, one of the many saloons in Jerome:

On a particular day, I believe in 1909, David Schreiber was attempting to collect the rent for the Beer Hall, which he owned. However, David was drunk and stumbled into the wrong bar, Otto's Place, where Otto's young nephew Walter was tending bar. David Schreiber walked in and demanded the rent. Walter knew he was in the wrong bar and tried to explain. David wasn't hearing it and grabbed Walter by the neck and shot him dead at close range. Walter was twenty-one years old. There was a pursuit by police, and they chased David all the way up to the Montana Hotel and shot him dead on the grand stairway.

An interesting notice was posted by Marshall J.W. Blankenship in November 1899 in an attempt to clean up this growing wicked city:

All able bodied persons not having visible means to maintain themselves and who live daily without employment or who are found loitering around and lodging in drinking saloons, bar-rooms, outhouses, houses of bad repute or any public places, such as sidewalks, street, alleys, vacant lots, plazas or parks or sheds, wagons or boxes, or who shall be found trespassing upon private premises without being able to give satisfactory account of themselves or who shall go from house to house or upon the street or any other place in said town begging for themselves or who habitually loiters or hangs around saloons, bar-rooms, bawdy houses and lives without visible means of support, will be arrested and placed in the chain-gang at labor on the streets of the Town of Jerome after 24 hours posting of this notice.

Jerome also experienced multiple fires that destroyed significant areas of town. However, strong spirit that Jerome has, it would always rebuild. The fire of 1899 was responsible for prompting Jerome to incorporate, create the volunteer fire department and adopt strict building codes that required brick or masonry construction.

The Jerome business district burned to the ground four times between 1894 and 1899. In 1894, a block or two in the business district burned; on December 24, 1897, twelve buildings were destroyed; on September 11, 1898, a fire destroyed all of Jerome's business district and half the residences. And this is how the *Arizona Weekly Journal-Miner* published the front-page news on September 14, 1898:

DEATH AND DESOLATION: The Greatest Disaster that Has Ever Occurred in Arizona Follows the Fire Which Wiped the Town of Jerome Out of Existence Sunday Morning. In Addition to a Property Loss of Half a Million Dollars, the Horrors of the Catastrophe Are Intensified by the Frightful Loss of Human Lives…CIGARETTES! WHISKEY!! AND GASOLINE!!!

Many stories circulated as to the origin of the fire, including one that blamed it on a "blow out" that night when at a gathering of carousing men someone threw lit cigarettes into a pile of wastepaper near a gasoline can, which caused an explosion and set the building on fire.

The fire of 1897 started behind the Connor Hotel on Christmas Eve. Evidently, a prostitute became angry with her customer and threw a kerosene lantern at him that caused an uncontrollable fire, and there was no fire department at the time. Twelve buildings made of wood and canvas burned, including four saloons, two restaurants and several houses of ill repute.

One alleged cause of the great fire of September 11, 1898, was that it started when a drunken Austrian living on Hull Avenue, just below Main Street, put too much kerosene in his stove. This caused an uncontrollable fire that leveled the entire business district. The fire spread all the way to the Hogback, a half mile away. Forty people were reported missing, with ten confirmed deaths. This is the incident when the infamous madam Jennie Bauters ran out into the street and offered the firemen "favors for life" if they saved her building.

Then, on May 19, 1899, forty dwellings burned. This destructive fire started on First Avenue in the Leland Hotel. Once again, the wooden buildings caught fire immediately. The newly formed town council soon passed an ordinance requiring all buildings on Main Street to be made out of nonflammable materials.

A particularly devastating fire struck one of Jerome's most elegant gems on February 28, 1915, when the luxurious and massive Montana Hotel burned to the ground, despite being constructed of brick. It towered over the town from Company Hill, next to the mine's open pit. Oddly enough, Clark built it for the miners.

The Mexicantown fire of 1918 occurred when Jerome finally had a fire department, but unfortunately, the hoses were too short to fight it. The fire blew back on itself and destroyed the lower part of Hull Avenue, where the Wigwam Saloon, Nevada Saloon, a Chinese laundry, a bottling plant and a plumbing business were all located. One hundred structures in all were destroyed; however, the business district was saved.

Fires roared out of control in 1918 in some of the mine shafts. One of the mine fires at United Verde burned for more than twenty years and prompted Senator Clark to switch to open pit mining.

April 1905 saw a mine explosion in Jerome. The accident happened as one shift was ending, so most men were already out of the mining shaft. It is believed that the recent heavy rains had found their way to an area of the mine where the fire had been smoldering for years. Steam was generated and caused the explosion, blowing out the bulkheads that were installed to

The Montana Hotel, built out of stone in 1900 to house miners. It burned to the ground in 1915. *Courtesy Jerome Historical Society.*

The block on the left was destroyed when a large underground blast damaged the business district. *Courtesy Jerome Historical Society.*

prevent the flames from spreading. Several lives were lost by suffocation from smoke and heated steam.

In addition to the fires, accidents and murders, several devastating epidemics ran through Jerome, ending in many fatalities. The first recorded was a typhoid epidemic in 1891, and then it returned to wreak more devastation in 1900. The smallpox epidemic of 1901 followed and filled the "pest house" that they had constructed several miles downhill from town, where those who had fallen ill were quarantined.

The 1918 epidemic was the worst. One alleged claim is that during the time of the 1918 Spanish influenza, so many bodies piled up they began burning them in the smelter to dispose of the quantities and keep the outbreak from being worse.

In an effort to curb the spread of disease, an ordinance was passed by the mayor and common council of the town of Jerome on December 11, 1917, prohibiting expectoration on sidewalks:

> SECTION 1. *It shall be unlawful for any person, or persons, to spit or expectorate upon any of the public sidewalks, or cross walks, or upon the floor, or upon the steps of any public building within the corporate lmits [sic] of the Town of Jerome.*

> SECTION 2. *Any person who shall violate the provisions of this ordinance, shall be deemed guilty of a misdemeanor, and shall, upon conviction, be fined not less than Five Dollars and not more than Fifty Dollars, or imprisoned in the Town Jail for not less than five days nor more than 30 days.*

Another severe smallpox epidemic followed in 1924. There were no high school graduation ceremonies in 1924. High school boys reported as guards to prevent people from leaving Jerome. Dr. James M. Coleman said that ninety-nine out of one hundred of his patients in Jerome did not have bathtubs, which was one reason why the epidemic was so widespread. Activities were suspended—no athletic events, dances or theatrical performances were held.

With the numerous mining accidents, fires, murders, diseases and overdoses, William Munds, the mayor of Jerome, signed into effect Ordinance No. 2, Section 26, on March 21, 1899. As quoted in Rabago's book, the Jerome ordinance read: "No person who is diseased, maimed, mutilated or in any way deformed, so as to be unsightly or disgusting object or an improper person, to be allowed in or on the streets, highways, thoroughfares or public places in this

Jerome suffered several epidemics. People were advised to wear masks, and public gatherings were forbidden. Hundreds died. *Courtesy Jerome Historical Society.*

Town, shall not therein or thereon expose himself or herself to public view." This was an extremely cruel ordinance.

Considering the number of accidents that resulted in crippled men, the ordinance condemned them to poverty and struggle and kept the new miners signing up to work in the mines from seeing the crippled men. Visit Jerome and you'll find many back alleyways and stairways in town.

It's no surprise that so many spirits cling to this mountainside town—so many untimely deaths! After working on this project and hearing one spirit experience after another, I can tell you that there is definitely something going on in Jerome. The spirits can touch you, turn lights on and off, turn on gas stoves and faucets, make items of all sizes move or disappear, disable your car, move your furniture, talk with you, make phone calls and open and close doors. These phenomena occur throughout Jerome.

This seems an appropriate place to share a fun experience Patricia had in Jerome before she moved here:

The first time I went to Jerome was in 1971. I was camping with some friends in a nearby canyon. We discovered we had forgotten the food on the kitchen table back in Tempe. A classic "I thought you got it…no, I thought you got it." Anyway, we were starving! We saw the twinkling lights of Jerome up on the hill and drove up the mountain, hoping and praying that something would be there with food. When we turned the corner to the only stop sign in town, we saw him. It was the last Chinese restaurant in Jerome. It was called the English Kitchen, and the owner was standing in the doorway. He was

Artist rendering, oil: *Paul and Jerry's Saloon*. Otto's Place on the right. The Chinese tunnels are exposed here. *Copyright Cody DeLong.*

backlit, and he looked like an angel dressed all in white. Oh boy, Chinese food! We were so hungry. He seemed to be very happy to see people, even though we were college kids. He brought us a menu that had many Chinese dishes on it. We ordered, and he scribbled on his pad and smiled. He went to the back and returned shortly. He sat at the counter across from our booth and asked us many questions. It seemed he hadn't seen any strangers in a very long time. We had a great time talking with him and then he disappeared into the back. He then came out with the food and with a funny laugh he said, "Chop suey, chop suey, chop suey, chop suey!" We quickly understood that was all he had, and we were in a ghost town where he always cooked one pot of food for the handful of people who were still in this ghost town!

At one time, there were twenty-seven Chinese restaurants in Jerome. Built in 1899, the English Kitchen (now Bobby D's BBQ) is one of the originals still standing today. It was once called Charlie Hong's. After the last owner of the English Kitchen died, the Jerome residents apparently found an opium den in the cellar and the remains of tunnels that seemed to originate there. There is evidence they were used during Prohibition, although they are all caved in now.

THERE IS NO CURE FOR DEATH

THE JEROME GRAND HOTEL ON HILL STREET

A s you drive up the highway from Cottonwood to Jerome, the massive building you can't help but notice on the mountain is the majestic Jerome Grand Hotel. At night, you can clearly see the twinkling lights of Jerome and the Grand Hotel across the Verde Valley from Sedona.

The Grand Hotel, formerly known as the United Verde Hospital, was originally built in 1926. It replaced the old hospital built in 1917 to care for sick and injured miners. It was constructed when a fault shift, due to blasting, damaged the south wing of the third hospital. What is now the Grand was the fourth hospital built in Jerome, known as the most modern and well-equipped hospital in the state of Arizona at the time. The hospital featured laboratories; X-ray machines; major and minor surgery facilities; separate wards for men, women and children; private and semiprivate rooms; patient call lights, balconies and sun porches; emergency backup lighting; an Otis self-service elevator; an icemaking room; and even blanket warming closets and housing for some staff.

Phelps Dodge Mining Corporation acquired the United Verde Jerome Mine holdings in 1935 and continued to operate the United Verde Hospital until its closing in 1950. The hospital was maintained fully furnished for about twenty years, after which Phelps Dodge knew it would never be used as a hospital again. Most of the furnishings were removed in the 1970s and '80s, and Phelps Dodge would, over time, hire a live-in caretaker or lease it to a family just to keep it occupied and safe from vandals. After the suicidal death of the last caretaker in the 1980s, the building was boarded up and

Left: The Jerome Grand Hotel, the most haunted building in Arizona. *Copyright Michael Thompson.*

Below: Current photograph of the Jerome Grand Hotel, formerly the United Verde Hospital. *Copyright Ron Chilston.*

watched over by the local police and a small staff still at the Phelps Dodge headquarters in Jerome.

The old hospital building sat idle for the next forty-four years until May 29, 1994, when it was purchased by the enterprising Larry Altherr, who held the fabulous vision of renovation and repurposed it to become the Grand Hotel. We are all glad he did!

A reported nine thousand people died during its twenty-four short years as a hospital, about one death for each day the hospital was opened. That is a lot of pain, sickness and death! It appears that some of the thousands who suffered and then died in this building chose to remain here in Jerome as spirits haunting these rooms and halls.

Longtime Jerome resident and author Roberto Rabago made a good point in *Rich Town Poor Town*:

> *Keep in mind that the world of Jerome a century ago was a completely different world than today's world. Then, there were no labor unions, no Fair Labor Standards Act, no OSHA, no antidiscrimination laws, no welfare, no worker's compensation, no minimum wage, no unemployment insurance, on and on. Neither did a world of independent law and justice exist, because the all-powerful mining companies were not restrained in any way by the regulations and laws that did exist. The mining companies were the law.*

SPIRITS

Who are these spirits at the Grand Hotel? With all the fires, accidents, murders and illnesses during Jerome's boomtown days, it's no wonder so many accounts exist of paranormal activity here.

Try to imagine Jerome at the height of its mining days. Local past employee of the Jerome Historical Society and well-respected resident Jessica said it well:

> *I have researched a lot of what went down here about mining and the deaths. These men led such tortured lives. They were working underground for twelve hours a day and treated as though their lives were expendable. The time and money they did have after working really hard for it, was spent on avoidance—prostitution and alcohol. They were just really unhappy and worked to the bone. They endured a lot of trauma and then died so fast their soul and life force didn't really get a chance to understand what happened and didn't get a chance to right how it had been wronged. They just stayed*

The United Verde Hospital was built in 1926 after a mine blast damaged the previous hospital. *Courtesy Jerome Historical Society.*

The Hampton House. Originally the second Jerome hospital, it was repurposed to house nurses and mine workers. It is now gone. *Courtesy Jerome Historical Society.*

here and lingered because they didn't get the proper chariot to move back into the collective soul. They got stuck here.

In addition to all the patients who died at the United Verde Hospital from mining accidents and illnesses, several suicides and a possible murder also occurred in the infamous building.

Claude Harvey was killed when his head was reportedly caught underneath the hospital elevator on April 3, 1935. Many folks actually believe this was a planned assassination—that Harvey was murdered elsewhere and then placed under the elevator to make it look like an accident.

Two maintenance men hanged themselves in the boiler room. One was in 1980 after the hospital was abandoned. He was discovered and cut down from his noose by our beloved retired police chief, Ron Ballatore.

A woman named Gurthie jumped to her death from the third floor—reason unknown.

A man in a wheelchair fell to his death from one of the upper balconies. His name is unknown. This is also believed to have been a possible suicide.

In *Rich Town Poor Town*, Roberto told a heartbreaking story of a man named Juan whose legs were burned off in the smelter. Before Juan could heal, he was thrown out of the hospital. Dr. Murietta delivered Juan a good supply of morphine and told him that it was all right to take extra if he was in horrible pain. Juan lived in Mexicantown. The doctor proceeded to walk down the hill to the train in Clarkdale from there; he couldn't work for those heartless people any longer. Juan died a few days later by taking his own life with an overdose of the pain medication that the good doctor left him. Roberto noted that the mine was known to withhold medical care if it appeared the injured miner would never return to productive service, especially if they were of Mexican heritage. This was the apparent case with Juan: he was discharged without being healed and with no means of caring for himself. He was discharged to die.

Rabago explained:

At some point it became apparent to the people in control, the ones who were managing the money, that mining was a business in which accidents and deaths occurred quite often. They realized that those deaths and accidents directly affected the margin of profit, and that they could never make as much profit as they wanted to make if they had to take long-term care of injured miners, especially those with no hope of recovery....They didn't kill outright, but they just left many to die of neglect. Sometimes they paid a small sum to the family of miners, enough to pay their way out of town. This gave the company a fixed cost that was included as part of the operating cost of the mining business. A death was followed by a simple bookkeeping entry.

So many spirit sightings and experiences have happened at the Grand Hotel, the most haunted structure in Arizona, that we've divided them up by floors. These are accounts from personal interviews conducted in 2018, as well as web research, and represent only a small slice of all the spirit encounters in Jerome. The Grand Hotel keeps logbooks in the lobby in which guests can record their haunting experiences, and they quickly fill several books every year.

THE BASEMENT AND LOBBY

The Grand Hotel's longtime head housekeeper, Cindy, has had the most spirit encounters at the hotel from her many years of working there. She can tell several stories about the boiler room alone:

Down in the boiler room we have a little breakroom, a bathroom, a storage unit and the general manager's office. Apparently, one of the maintenance workers hung himself there. When I first started working at the Grand, they had the original rope still hanging from the pipe. Eventually, they took the rope down. One day I went into the bathroom and had a cigarette lit. In this bathroom, the sink is practically in front of the toilet. I put my cigarette on the edge of the sink. It literally levitated and then set back down. I couldn't run out of that bathroom fast enough! I actually ran out with my pants down!

During the dead season (no pun intended), Cindy was there by herself and feeling fine. She was taking the laundry down into the boiler room when all of a sudden she felt feverish, like she had pneumonia or something. Cindy grabbed her head and said aloud, "I don't feel so good." She suddenly felt someone breathe in her ear and heard a chuckle. She looked around to see if she was there by herself. She said the chuckle was like a soft whisper, and she could feel the breath in her ear. Then the spirit laughed!

Cindy also reported that things would disappear. She would place her items in one spot, and seconds later, they weren't there. They would reappear in the oddest places, places she knew she'd never think of putting her things. Working at the Grand Hotel keeps her on her toes!

One time, Cindy was down in the boiler room with her supervisor; they were standing by the time clock. Cindy saw the face of a man standing behind her supervisor. It was just a face. Cindy was trying to listen to her supervisor, but she was distracted and told her supervisor a face was behind her. Her supervisor wouldn't turn around—she refused to hear it!

Spirit cats have also been reported at the Grand Hotel. Apparently, an old custom was to employ cats in hospitals because they were believed to have the ability to sense when someone may be close to death and help alert the nurses.

Steve, a front desk night clerk, told of a guest who brought his own pillow and discovered cat paw prints imprinted on it during the night!

Steve has had several encounters with spiritual entities at the Grand. One evening, while working the lobby reception desk, Steve, there all alone, witnessed a stack of trays suddenly flung to the floor. He put them back where they belonged and then shook the counter to see if he could re-create what happened, but he could only get them to creep a few fractions of an inch. It was virtually impossible for the stack of trays to crash to the floor without physical effort from somewhere or someone.

One night, Steve was heading to the back storage room when a moving shadow crossed over a path of light in front of him and then disappeared into the "cooler room." The cooler room is theorized to have been the morgue of the United Verde Hospital. Steve looked into the room, but there was nobody there. He retraced his steps to see if he could see the moving shadow again. No shadow.

Steve has felt a spirit presence of some sort in the back storage room more than once, where he was sure he was being watched. Perhaps the moving shadow? He has checked up to six times in one night for someone watching him, and there was never anyone there.

The Third Floor

The third floor is where the operating room was located and where most of the deaths occurred. Can you handle a night in a haunted hotel famous for its paranormal activity? For a real thrill, book yourself into room 32. Some believe it is the room most frequented by the spirits.

Another experience happened to Steve when he and his wife were staying in room 32. At about three o'clock in the morning, Steve suddenly felt like he was sitting on a rollercoaster and then felt a sharp pain in the back of his head, followed immediately by the sensation of wetness on his head.

He brought his arms up to touch the moisture, but his head was dry. Steve speculated that he was experiencing what may have happened to a miner who was brought to the hospital; that perhaps the miner was in a mining cart (the rollercoaster ride) when he was suddenly hit by an object (the sharp pain) and rushed to the hospital where he bled out and died (the wetness on his head). There were so many horrific mine accidents it would be impossible to trace whose spirit this was.

Steve and another Grand Hotel employee related a story of a housekeeper who when checking under the bed in room 32 felt a clear push on her shoulder. She shrugged it off. She then went to the other side of the bed to check underneath it and felt an even stronger push on her shoulder. She relayed this story to one of the night staff, who checked her shoulder, only to find fingertips imprinted there.

A real spine-tingling, hair-raising spirit experience happened to Cindy, the longtime head housekeeper of the Grand Hotel. "I was looking for a job, and I was told that the Jerome Grand Hotel was hiring. I didn't know anything about the hotel whatsoever. I just wanted a job, and I thought it would be interesting because I have always been intrigued by Jerome's history."

Cindy had her first spirit experience about three months after starting to work at the Grand. There was an antique table mirror in the workstation on the third floor. She needed a clean tablecloth and went up to the workstation to get one. When she went in, she noticed something dark swaying back and forth in the mirror. She looked directly in the mirror, but it wasn't her face reflected back. It was the face of a man covered in purple, black and blue abrasions. He looked like he had been beaten to death. His eyes were beet red and actually poking out of his face. Cindy thought it was some kind of trick being played on her. She began looking for gadgets in the mirror. She looked in the mirror again and saw nothing. She couldn't believe that moments before she had seen an apparition. She took the mirror straight down to the front desk and told the clerk, "I want to throw his away. Something bizarre just happened to me. You can keep the mirror down here but I don't want it up there." The very next day, she was working on the second floor. She was cleaning a large wall mirror when suddenly the same spirit face she had seen in the workstation appeared again, this time behind her!

Cindy immediately started looking for another job. She applied and applied, but no other jobs surfaced. She had never had a problem finding employment before. Cindy had to continue working at the Grand Hotel, even though she dreaded it. To get through it, she focused on being the new girl, doing a good job and going home. She never read any of the logbooks, even though she knew they were there for guests to share their own ghostly experiences.

Not long after this first encounter, the same spirit entity of the grotesque man actually followed her home. Cindy had to have her house blessed three different times before it stopped.

A few months into working at the Grand, she was on the second floor and heard a scream. One of her coworkers ran down from the third floor, visibly shaken. "Cindy you have to come hear this." She went up to the third floor, where a frightened young woman had fled from her room, terrified. She had woken up that morning and was about to get dressed when she looked in the mirror and saw precisely what Cindy had seen a few months earlier. She was in a skimpy nightgown, freaked out, and the gathering crowd in the hotel hallway was trying to calm her down. As she was describing to everyone what she had seen, Cindy was listening and agreeing with every bit of it. She felt wrong saying it, but Cindy said the spirit looked like a creature right out of a horror movie. That's how bad he looked, and the young guest described it to a "T." She perfectly described exactly what Cindy had seen. That was her first experience with a spirit, and to this day she will never forget it. It was crystal clear to her.

Later on, Cindy heard stories about Claude Harvey and thought, "Oh my god, I bet that beaten creature was him." Harvey was a maintenance man at the United Verde Hospital, and he really liked one particular nurse who worked there. He didn't like the way she was being treated and got himself involved. Cindy heard that he was murdered elsewhere, brought to the hospital and positioned under the elevator, where it took his head off to cover up the murder. The spirit entity in the mirror was just the head. There was no body.

Cindy's next spirit experience happened when she was assigned to room 26 on the second floor. It was during the slow season. Cindy was the only housekeeper there, along with one front desk person. All guests were checked out, and she only had four rooms to clean. She was in room 26 making the beds when she heard a conversation that sounded like it was from far away, as if from another dimension. From what Cindy could tell, two people were tied up, and a male voice told them, "You move one more time, and I'll cut your throats." Cindy clearly heard every word, even though it sounded far away—she knew it was not her imagination. She walked up and down the halls checking every room. She finally went down to the front desk and asked the clerk if anybody had been in the hotel in the last hour. No one had. The voice was crystal clear, but it sounded as though it was coming from a different realm. Cindy said that she will never forget it.

Despite these scary encounters, Cindy booked two rooms at the Grand Hotel for family who were coming to visit: rooms 39A and 39B, when they were a connected suite, not two separate rooms as they are today. She put her family in 39A, and she and her ex-husband stayed in 39B. Cindy always felt weird in that room; it was dark and she didn't like the way it made her feel. She and her ex-husband ended up in room 39A with the family, where it was light and bright.

The curtains were open and the streetlight was shining in the room as she was getting ready for bed when suddenly she felt a hand pushing her head into the mattress. She opened her eyes and saw a black mass around her face. Scared, she turned around and looked at her ex-husband, whose eyes were demon red with black crosses popping out of his face! She threw the blankets over her head and stayed up all night long.

It was tough work when Cindy first started working at the Grand. They had only one part-time and two full-time housekeepers in charge of cleaning twenty-five rooms. It was a crazy and exhausting schedule to keep. Cindy was assigned to 37B, and when she walked in, she saw a white mist in the middle of the room. She thought it was her tired eyes playing tricks on her. There was no draft and nothing to explain it. She was walking toward it when all of a sudden Cindy's hair blew back, and the spirit entity went right through her! Cindy turned around and ran out of the room just as she felt it get ice cold for half a second. As time went on, she heard several stories about things happening in that room.

Cindy also related an extraordinary experience that happened in room 38 one day when she was the only one on the third floor. The hotel policy is that anytime guests check out, the room needs to be opened immediately to let it air out. Cindy was getting ready to clean room 38 when she saw a man walking by. She can remember exactly what he was wearing: a shirt and jeans and a ballcap. He went into room 37A, two doors down the hall from her. She thought perhaps he was a guest who had forgotten something, so she quickly followed him to see if she could be of assistance. The only way in or out of room 37A is through the door to the hall. As soon as she entered the room, nobody was there. Now, if someone needed to escape, they could jump off the balcony or go through the door. But not enough time had passed for this man to do either. The room was empty just seconds after the man had entered the room.

Two weeks later, Cindy was working on the second floor when a coworker said they needed her help. A guest was unresponsive, and his wife was hysterical. When Cindy got to the room, two hotel guests, professional nurses, were giving the man CPR. They asked Cindy to hold his feet. She immediately recognized the man's ballcap, jeans and shirt. She looked at him and realized that she had seen the same man—what must have been his spirit entity—walking into room 37A two weeks earlier. And there in front of her that day was his physical entity, dead from a heart attack in room 37A.

Cindy smiled as she recalled one spirit entity with a sense of humor, although she didn't find it very funny in the moment. She was about to clean the bathroom in suite 39A and B. As she was standing there, deciding what she needed to do first, she felt her shirt literally pulled off her shoulder. She was alone. Then the shower curtain unexpectedly jutted out as if pulled or poked by someone. Then her shirt was jutting out. Cindy pushed her shirt down, but the shower curtain stayed sticking straight out! Cindy walked out of the room, counted to ten and walked back in. The prank was over.

Cindy recently had the same thing happen on two separate occasions in room 36. She was airing out the room and assessing how she wanted to start cleaning when she felt a sharp pain on the back of her shoulder. "Ow! Really?" she exclaimed, and shrugged it off. Later on at home, as she was stepping out of the shower, she happened to look in the full-length mirror in her bathroom and noticed a dark welt on her shoulder. She couldn't believe what she was seeing. It was a bruise shaped like a fist. She could even make out a knuckle imprint. Something had punched her in room 36! Twice!

The Grand Suite is another room that has spooked Cindy. The double refrigerator in the Grand Suite has doors that can be opened and locked into place. While she was inspecting it, Cindy felt an abrupt pressure from behind. The left door had slammed into her and almost knocked her into the refrigerator! The doors had been locked in place.

Cindy's last eerie experience as of this writing happened on the third floor. A man in a wheelchair had apparently committed suicide in room 32. Cindy had never had trouble in there before, but one day, just as she walked in to clean the room, the glass chandelier began to spin out of control! Only an industrial fan or incredible windstorm could blow it that hard, but there was no fan, no open windows, no storm. Cindy stood watching it in disbelief.

THE ASYLUM RESTAURANT

The Asylum Restaurant is located in what used to be the hospital reception area. A woman we'll call Simone worked nine years at the Asylum. She had several hair-raising stories to share.

Many Jerome visitors go to the Asylum—skeptics looking for spirit experiences at the most haunted place in Arizona. Simone would simply tell them, "It may happen…but we can't really make you believe." One late evening, two guys and a gal were drinking at the bar, chatting with the staff. Simone doesn't think anyone else was in the restaurant. The Asylum employees were sharing their spirit experiences with the doubting visitors. The two guys had their beers on the bar; they were sitting, and the young woman was standing. Simone told them if they were only here for one day they're probably not going to notice anything anyway; besides, they don't have to believe. Just then, the first guy's beer tipped over when he wasn't touching it. The second guy's beer tipped over right after, and then the woman's necklace came undone! They accused Simone of having a switch under the bar. She just smiled and told them, "The spirits are just letting you know not to be skeptics." The woman's necklace had a spring-ring clasp that could only release using two hands. She screamed at the sensation of her jewelry falling off. Simone would often wear chopsticks in her hair, and the spirits would pull the chopsticks out and fly them around the room! Simone knew it was the mischievous spirits playing tricks with the visitors because they would do the same thing to her.

Simone also told of a spirit cat the restaurant workers would often feel rubbing against their legs; they even had sightings of it walking in the hall. One time, Simone took a photo of some guests at their dinner table, and there was the cat, sitting on the table. The guests looked at the photo and were startled to see the cat. The same thing happened with a photo in the hallway. Someone was photographing the hallway when a server, just a server, was walking into the kitchen, and right behind the server was a cat. But only in the photo.

The spirit of a young boy would also hang around the bar and leave his handprints on the windows. The staff would blame Simone because she had small hands. But it wasn't Simone; she had to clean those windows, so she wouldn't do that. The little boy spirit was often seen around the bar and in the room next to the main dining room.

Another photographic mystery happened with people sitting at one of the tables—perhaps 11 or 13. Behind them was an abstract painting on the wall. One of the patrons asked Simone if she would take a picture of her and her partner, and she happily obliged. They weren't pleased with the first photo, so they asked her to take another. Something was different in the second photo, but at first they couldn't figure out what. Then they realized that this time the painting was upside down. No one had even touched the painting—certainly not in the few seconds between the two snapshots.

Simone has seen the spirit of a man several times in the hallway and in the elevator, wearing a top hat and spectacles. A few times, she thought she saw him running down the stairs to the lobby, his coattails flying behind him. Two or three times she followed him, but by the time she reached the lobby, he'd be gone. The person at the front desk never saw him. Most of these spirit sightings have occurred in the evening, during the dinner shift or at the end of the shift.

Simone's last spirit experience at the Grand Hotel happened in the bathroom of the Asylum. It was originally the bathroom for minor surgery. It still had the same tile. She was working one night and went into the stall when she realized that there was no toilet paper. She decided to sit and wait, in the hopes that one of her coworkers would come in and help her out. As she waited, a roll of toilet paper suddenly rolled into her stall! No one had come into the bathroom. Despite the creepy energy, Simone thanked the spirits, finished her business and left.

A little Mexican lady worked as chef in the Asylum and would mention the "bad spirits." She would be preparing these beautiful dishes, and the spirits would slap them out of her hand. Simone remembered the day she quit. The chef said the spirits were "pushing her towards the fryer" and that she couldn't work there anymore. She had worked there for a long time and was known to have done a great job but she got sick of fighting the spirits just to make food.

Ellen related an experience she had when she was working as a bartender at the Asylum. All the staff wore black and white. She noticed a young woman behind the bar wearing black and white and wondered who she was. A new employee? She seemed to be in her early twenties, but Ellen could only see the top half of her body. The woman had on a high-collared blouse and what looked like a bodice to a long dress or skirt. The woman had most of her back to Ellen, but she appeared to be looking through files. Behind the bar? The reader may recall that this part of the Asylum used to be the hospital reception area, with a massive desk to the left and the clerks' station to the right (now the bar), with offices beyond. The rest of the room was a waiting room. Ellen said that the woman was fully formed, not transparent, and looked like a real person. Ellen decided to approach her, and as she did, the woman turned away and went into the back room, where there was no other exit. When Ellen entered the room, nobody was there. Who could this have been? The spirit of a hospital staff member who became sick and died unexpectedly? The spirit going through files made perfect sense.

Patricia told a fun personal story about the United Verde Hospital after it closed in 1953:

After the mines closed, the hospital quickly became obsolete. The mining company and the state decided to keep the hospital intact in case of an emergency. They created an apartment in the old hospital in 1983 to keep out the vandals. The guy who had the apartment in the hospital had about two dozen pairs of skates and a great reel-to-reel, very loud stereo. We skated to bubble gum music, in and out of pre-op, the actual operating room, sterilization rooms, the recovery room and across the balcony. All the equipment was still there, including the operating table and its special light! What a gas!

Our town librarian, the beautiful Ms. Kathleen, shared an experience she had with her boyfriend at the time before the hospital was turned into the Grand Hotel:

Harvey was my boyfriend at the time. We were together from 1993 to 1996, and then he died. So this incident would have happened in '94. It was right after Larry bought the building. It was still the abandoned hospital before they started to repurpose it and turn it into the Grand. He had an open-house weekend to allow the public, basically the town people, to go up and just wander around, to see the old place one more time. It was so freaking spooky. It was empty and in very poor repair—peeling paint on the ceilings and walls and that sort of thing.

First of all, let me explain a little bit about Harvey, so you will understand why what I am about to tell you was so unusual: He was a New York businessman before he came to Jerome. I mean, he was conservative, in control of himself. He would call himself "Suit." He was the Suit because he wore a suit to work and he told everybody what to do. He owned a business. He came to Jerome to pursue his dream of being an artist. He was a woodcarver, and he was an excellent woodcarver. He had real talent.

So, Harvey and I were wandering around the old hospital. We were in there about an hour or so. We were up on the surgical floor near one end of the building…and Harvey briefly walked away from me to another part of the area on the floor. When he came back to my side, he was crying, which doesn't happen with a New York suit man—never. He couldn't talk to me. He couldn't tell me why. Of course I was very, very upset. What could possibly be going on? This is not the man I know. Later in the day, he was able to speak about it. He told me that he had died in that hospital from a chest injury, and he knew it when he was walking around by himself on the floor! Now, you want to call that a ghost story? I would put that in the category. He never talked about it anymore after that. He went back to being Suit. Not "the Suit" but "Suit."

The Party Continues

The Clubhouse on Hill Street

Located just a short distance down the street from the Jerome Grand Hotel sits what is now called the Clubhouse. It was initially constructed in 1917 by the United Verde Mining Company and served as Jerome's third hospital until 1927, when the new United Verde Hospital was built (now the Grand Hotel).

The Spanish influenza victims of 1918 were taken to this hospital and then later to the back of the building and, eventually, the morgue. It is said that more than one hundred citizens were affected by the influenza. Victims of shootings, fires and mining accidents were taken care of in the operating room on the third floor.

In 1928, the facility was transformed into the Jerome Public Library and Clubhouse. An estimated seven thousand books were on the ground floor. The *Mining Congress Journal* did a feature on the facility in 1930, which had a card room, a soda fountain and a pool table, among other niceties.

The south wing of the facility was destroyed during an earthquake in 1927. The retaining wall was cracked in 1934 with the movement of the Verde fault.

Spirits

On the horror-themed website 13thfloor, the Clubhouse is mentioned in its story about the "Wickedest City in the West." Some say it's the most haunted building in Jerome:

In the background you can see the third hospital being built, now called the Clubhouse. Ghost City Inn in the left foreground. *Courtesy Jerome Historical Society.*

During nights of the full moon, ghosts of former patients can be seen in the windows of the abandoned building. Patients of this facility were largely miners who suffered terrible accidents while on the job. They were rushed into the hospital to be operated on, which mostly meant losing a limb. During the great Spanish influenza epidemic of 1918, the hospital was so crowded that incinerators were constantly burning to dispose of the massive amount of bodies.

The Clubhouse building was featured in an episode of *Ghost Adventures* in 2011, a popular television series about the paranormal. Lonnie is a master carpenter who used to have his highly respected carpentry shop on the ground floor of the Clubhouse. During his interview in the *Ghost Adventures* episode, you can hear a door slam shut when there is nobody near the door, and the weather is perfectly calm outside.

Lonnie also told of an experience he had while he was washing out some of his paintbrushes. He had to leave his shop and walk down the hall past the morgue (where the incinerator was still full of ashes from the burned bodies of the former patients) to get to the sink to wash his brushes. All of a sudden, Lonnie felt a presence, and the hair on his neck and arms stood up. He told the spirit that he was almost done and would be out of there soon.

Lonnie's wife, Renee, told a story of a time when Lonnie came home from working at the Clubhouse, and she was aware that he had a spirit follow him

Stairway to surgery in the Clubhouse. This hospital handled the Spanish influenza and was used from 1917 to 1926. *Copyright Michael Thompson.*

back. She asked Lonnie to return the ghost spirit to the Clubhouse, and she cleared the space at home.

Longtime Jerome residents and past owners of the Clubhouse building Vanessa and Tony have told me about their ghost encounters at the former hospital. One of Vanessa's old friends was a tenant in the building and had a young daughter who liked to play with an "imaginary friend." One day, this little girl came to her parents and told them that she didn't think she wanted to be friends with her anymore because her "imaginary" friend wanted her to "fly from the balcony" so they could be together forever.

Vanessa would occasionally have yard sales in front of the Clubhouse. On one occasion, she was selling some of her daughter's childhood items she had outgrown and toys she didn't want anymore. A man named Michael who was also renting from them bought some of the items for the young girl ghost that he would see on the third floor. Michael had never heard the story of the girl ghost that played with the other tenant's daughter.

Michael frequently saw a ghost of a man wearing Bermuda shorts, oddly enough. Others claimed to have seen the same oddly dressed spirit. According to Michael, "A spirit in Bermuda shorts is not a pleasant thing to encounter!" Michael established relationships with two or three spirits in the Clubhouse and left things for all of them depending on the nature of their character. Michael wasn't afraid of spirits. He wanted to accommodate them because he firmly believed in them.

The third United Verde Hospital in its heyday. *Courtesy Jerome Historical Society.*

Two women who reside in Jerome, Renee and Melissa, each have special skillsets when it comes to connecting with the spirits. Melissa said that spirits want people to know there is a way to help the stuck and disembodied to cross, go home and be free and happy once again—that it's not just about entertainment or thrill factor or all the things the TV shows are about. They are missing the point, which is to help them, and by helping them we support the whole planet because "when you are stuck, you are vibrating at a lower level, and that drains us all."

One day, Melissa was taking boxes up to the Clubhouse while waiting for her food to be ready at the Haunted Hamburger. She entered the storage area, what used to be the emergency room. Out of nowhere, a man wearing old scrubs and a nametag carrying a clipboard approached her. He told her that she was not allowed to be there, that it was a sterile environment for authorized personnel only. The spirit had his hand on the door. Melissa reassured him that everything was "cool," that she just needed to put her boxes down. She tried to explain to him that what was happening in that moment was actually happening in *his* time. She asked him if he remembered being in a body; he didn't know what she meant. She explained again about the moment in time, about being in a body. The spirit then put his hand on his heart and said, "No, not me. I didn't die. Everybody else was dying, but I didn't die. I am a doctor. I am saving them." Then he disappeared.

They met up several times over the next three weeks, and the spirit kept saying, "I think I am ready to go home." However, Melissa wasn't willing to call in the angels and open the portals unless he was really ready, until she heard him say, "I am ready." Melissa told the spirit that if he wasn't serious about going home, there was no point in talking anymore. The spirit went away for a few days, and when he returned, he was ready. Melissa called in the angels and opened the portal for him to pass. Melissa described it as if a floating orb were crossing over. A chamber opens in the middle of nowhere; the angels have him, life is beautiful and then they are gone. The spirit stepped into the chamber and said that he was going to see his son.

When Melissa told Lonnie about this, Lonnie presented a picture to her and asked if the spirit looked like the image in the photograph. Surprised, Melissa said it did, but the spirit wasn't dressed in a suit; he was dressed in scrubs. The image in the photograph was Don Walsh's father. He had lived in the brick house across the street from the Clubhouse; he was the hospital doctor at the time of the Spanish influenza. That is what the spirit meant when he said he was going to see his son. Don had brothers and sisters, but at that time, they had all passed except for Don.

HOME SWEET HOME

THE SURGEON'S HOUSE ON HILL STREET

The Surgeon's House was built in 1917 by the United Verde Copper Company for its chief surgeon, Dr. Lee Perry Kaull. It is an elegant Mediterranean-style mansion that includes all the modern-day comforts. The residence is now a very popular and upscale B&B that was lovingly renovated and restored to its original distinction by its current owner, Andrea Prince.

It is the authors' sincere desire that Andrea's remarkable heart and her dedication to the stewardship of this property be readily conveyed to the reader. She is truly a unique soul who respects and cherishes her humble position as the current "custodian" of the legacy of the Surgeon's House. We are blessed to have her here.

According to the Surgeon's House website, in the early 1930s, the house became the home of then chief surgeon, Dr. Arthur Carlson, and his family. Parties were often held at their home to "create a diversion for the company's upper echelon from their hard work in this hard rock mining town."

Most of Jerome was built on land from the original Hull homestead. The Hull residence was built on land that is now the side yard of the current Surgeon's House bed-and-breakfast.

SPIRITS

According to Andrea, perhaps seven or eight guests over the years have been awakened from sleep in the Maid's Suite Front to discover the apparition of a woman. She was slender, wearing a light-blue dress with a high neckline, her grayish-white hair piled up on her head. The apparition appeared to be patting or tucking someone into bed, as if she were just checking on them to see if they were all right.

It is Andrea's belief that we get our spiritual data as we ask for it and as it's meant to be revealed to us. She is a woman who receives impressions that are specifically disclosed to her from the other side. Andrea is uncertain as to the source of the information but believes that the woman's name was Alice and that Alice was a housekeeper in the Hull house, which remained in its original location until the Surgeon's House was completed. At that point, the Hull house was torn down. Andrea believes the reason the apparition only appeared to guests in that room was because Alice could see the Hull house from there.

The only personal experience Andrea has had with Alice was one night when she did not have any guests. She decided to sleep in the Maid's Suite Front, where the apparition had previously appeared, in the hopes that

This elegant Mediterranean-style residence was built by the United Verde to house the chief surgeon. *Courtesy Jerome Historical Society.*

she might experience it for herself. At that time, Andrea had two cats, Doc and Lulu. Doc and Lulu never slept together and never slept with Andrea. However, on that specific night, both cats nestled side by side on the corner of the bed, staring at the door. They didn't even sleep. They just sat there staring at the door. Andrea believes that cats are intuitive and instinctively knew that something else was going on.

Before going to sleep that night, Andrea said with intention, "OK, Alice, I am sleeping in your room tonight, and it would be nice if you would show yourself to me." Customarily, Andrea slept in the basement at the front of the Surgeon's House, where all the windows are. Sometime in the middle of the night, Andrea heard a woman's voice calling her name, "Andrea! Andrea!" She had no guests at the time and was confident that it was Alice calling up to her from the basement. Andrea replied, "No dice! I slept up here so that I could see you in the only place that you ever appear and now you're down there."

Andrea had one experience early on, before she was running the B&B and knew that no one should be coming into the house. One evening when she was by herself, sleeping in the Master Suite, she woke up to doors opening and the sound of footsteps. In her mind's eye, she saw the back door open and a man walk in. He put down his briefcase or perhaps a doctor's bag. The man had on a greatcoat and was walking as one would if they were trying to be quiet. He shut the door silently, walked through the kitchen and the dining room and then very quietly walked up the steps. He came into the Master Suite, where Andrea was, and closed the door. He then went into the bathroom and performed his ablutions. He came back into the bedroom and crawled into bed. How Andrea explained his presence was that she felt the need to hang on to the headboard. It was as if she were lying on the beach and a wave came in and rolled her. In fact, she rolled off the side of the bed, and then it was over!

Another experience that some of the guests have had when sleeping in the Master Suite was awakening in the night and seeing an apparition of a man and a woman dancing. Dr. Carlson's second wife used to conduct dance lessons at the Surgeon's House; the guests thought it was likely them. Andrea was not sure which doctor it might have been. When she conducted a research project several years ago, she discovered that four other doctors and bigwigs had also lived in the Surgeon's House.

Another time, guests were staying in the Master Suite. They were looking out the doors to the balcony toward the Clubhouse next door, at what resembled a greenhouse but had been, in fact, an operating room. They told Andrea the next morning that they had seen an apparition of a man standing there, staring back toward the Surgeon's House. The guests felt like he was staring specifically at them, through the original patio doors to the Master Suite balcony. They believed the man was a doctor. They watched each other for some time before the man suddenly turned and walked out of the operating room. No one has ever seen him since!

Andrea has had guests staying in the Chauffeur's Quarters who have asked her if she had a helper or someone who would have been coming up the stairs wearing fly-fishing gear. Andrea did not have a helper wearing that type of clothing. What a different sort of apparition that was! Whose spirit that might have been remains a complete wonder.

Another couple from San Francisco who stayed in the Master Suite had a curious experience with the apparition of a young child, perhaps seven or eight years of age. They saw the child peeking at them through the window in the door. The couple had been guests for several days when they asked Andrea if she had a little boy staying at the Surgeon's House.

Andrea has photographs hanging along the staircase guests take upstairs to get to their rooms. During their stay but before the guests had said anything to Andrea about the little boy, she would get up in the morning and all of the pictures in the stairwell would be crooked. After the guests started talking about the apparition, it was revealed that it was a little boy named Daniel.

Andrea believes that folks from the other side can latch on to someone and follow along with that person. They may think, "Oh, this is a good place. I will dump out here." Andrea has had to ask apparitions to leave. She very kindly told Daniel, "You can't be here, Daniel. You can't keep playing with my pictures. You can't be peeking at people in their suites."

One of the last experiences Andrea shared happened when she was sleeping in her private quarters in the basement. She would wake up to a whispering conversation. Andrea could never understand what they were saying, but she could definitely hear conversations.

It was revealed to her that a group of individuals was caught in a vortex underneath her house, near the steps. Andrea was puzzled as to how to help these spirits journey home, so she sought guidance from her spiritual teacher. She was told to repeat these words: "This is a place of light and love, and you are safe to leave, safe to go." Andrea did and started to hear more whispering.

Telling this part of the story made Andrea emotional. She recalled that the basement was dark, but she could see the spirits begin to leave—two, sometimes three at a time. The trapped spirits started coming up like puffs of smoke. "Go on, you are safe. Just move along," Andrea said to them. Perhaps sixty different spirits passed. Then, when there were five or six spirits remaining, she noticed that some of them were hiding. They were afraid. Andrea gently encouraged them. "Come on, you can't stay down here anymore. You have to go. It's safe." She could hear more whispering, and finally they were all free.

Years ago, when Andrea's dogs were still alive, a perfect circle of yellow grass appeared on her lush green lawn. At first she wondered if it was a favorite spot for them to do their business. But one day, when she saw the wind picking up, only the leaves above the circle were stirring.

About that time, people would come to her front door and say, "I don't know why I am here but I know I'm supposed to be here." It happened so frequently that Andrea questioned what was going on. She remembered having a woman show up who was experiencing a difficult pregnancy. The woman said, "I don't know why I am here, but I am supposed to be here. My baby and I are supposed to sit in the middle of your yard."

Andrea knows that she had a past life eons ago—right where she now lives in Jerome. She knows that somehow her home was choosing her as a completion of a circle. Mingus Mountain was a sacred place to the indigenous people. She learned that there had been a vortex right where the yellow circle appeared in her yard and that it was a sacred site.

Andrea takes the stewardship of her property and her business to heart. It is sacred to her.

COMPANY HILL AND A BIT MORE

O nly a few of the original houses still stand on Company Hill, on what used to be the bustling main road to the United Verde Mine, smelter and railroad. Now the road is cut off by the gigantic mining pit below. In fact, today you can still see how it was once paved with massive stones, not anything like the tiny cobbles used to pave roads back east. In the 1880s, it was the way to the small-gauge railroad situated at the top of Cleopatra Hill. It was also the passage many injured miners traveled down to get to the hospital.

The smelter was in Jerome until 1917, spewing noxious sulfur fumes. Company Hill was right next to it. William Andrews Clark, owner of the mine, moved the smelter down to Clarkdale, where he built the first housing development in the country for his smelter workers. This move was not for the comfort of the people on Company Hill but instead a move to exploit the copper ore under the smelter. The only way to get to that ore was to create the open pit because the ore body kept catching on fire.

The houses on Company Hill were ordered from Sears in Chicago and were shipped via the United Verde and Pacific Railway. The beautiful Victorian homes were put in place by 1897. Clark wanted his top executives very comfortable. The first hospital in Jerome had been built across the street, but it burned down in 1894. Some of the houses seem to have spirits that linger from that first hospital.

The people on Company Hill had nice homes but foul air and no sewage system until 1917. Everything flowed downhill. The air cleared up somewhat

A typical Company Hill house before restoration. All were Sears kit houses brought in by train in 1897. *Copyright Michael Thompson.*

after the smelter was moved five miles down the mountain. Company Hill was a genteel and privileged community. The new hospital, called the Hampton House, was opened on Main Street just below Company Hill. Another hospital was built on Hill Street in 1917, but alas, one of the wings of the hospital collapsed during a mine blast or earthquake (controversy of the times), so the hospital closed due to the instability. In 1926, the huge United Verde Hospital, now the Grand Hotel, was built both earthquake- and blast-proof.

ROSEMARY DECAMP HOUSE

A fabulous quote about the early days here is from Jerome's own Rosemary DeCamp, a famous movie star who grew up in Jerome: "The years we spent there remain in my memory as a mosaic of poverty, mine disasters, fires, picnics, wildly beautiful scenery, ugly houses, and strong, willful people."

In her memoir, *Tigers in My Lap*, DeCamp described the early days in the little mining town. She remembered that streets in Jerome were generally referred to as "rows." People lived on First Row, Second Row, Top Row or down on the Hogback. Shaky wooden sidewalks were constructed between the rows. Children were *never* to throw rocks, she recalled. The town seemed to cling to the side of the steep mountain.

This boardwalk was in front of the DeCamp house and went all the way to the mine.
Copyright Michael Thompson.

A long wooden sidewalk angled up to the mine. When the men came off shift, their boots could be heard thumping down the knotty old boards. When a mining accident happened, the men would carry the victims down the hill on stretchers. DeCamp can remember watching her mother's face as she listened, as when the workers were burdened, "the rhythm of their footsteps was different, regular, and ominous."

DeCamp wrote about witnessing a murder outside her window one day:

> *There were two churches on the long diagonal sidewalk. The old Episcopal Church was just below the end of our Row. The brick Catholic Church was right under our front window, about 100 feet away.*
>
> *I had a perpetual cold during those years, which was later diagnosed as tuberculosis, so I spent a lot of time on that window seat observing the entrance to the Catholic Church. All the meaningful life of Jerome seemed to be centered there: christenings, confirmations, funerals, weddings. It was rather like watching television today, looking down on that busy Catholic doorway. For a child watching alone, it made an indelible picture.*
>
> *One day I witnessed a jealous woman stab the best man at a wedding as the guests crowded out the narrow door. She killed the wrong man. Her intended victim, the groom, went off with his bride. The woman was left with the police, and the priest giving last rites to the dying boy.*

Patricia remembered the first time she came to Jerome and set eyes on the abandoned Company Hill houses. Stencils on the buildings warned "BEWARE OF RATTLESNAKES."

Patricia once stood in what was left of the DeCamp house at the time (now restored), in the living room by Rosemary's window. The entire place had filled with dirt that had crashed through the window in one of the great slides, and there was ivy growing inside the building. A round dishwasher from possibly the 1920s sat in the middle of the room.

SPIRITS

Walsh Apartments

Not far from Company Hill were the Walsh Apartments, directly across the street from the third hospital built in Jerome (now the Clubhouse). This next spirit experience happened to Scottie, a longtime Jerome resident and musician:

It was 1976 or '77 when I was playing music with a man named Bongo Billy—he was a drummer. It was him; my best buddy, Mick King, who was an excellent banjo picker; and myself. We were invited to Jerome to go to a birthday party as well as to play music. One thing led to another, and I wound up staying there for forty-seven years. During this time there was an apartment complex owned by Don Walsh, who has now since passed away. The complex had a long porch that went all the way to the back of the building. The main apartment had a big living space, a kitchen and a bathroom, and the last apartment had a door out to 89A. This experience happened in the middle of the summertime. The door was open to the main apartment. I walked down the porch, I turned, and I looked, and I saw the spirit of my buddy sitting on the floor all the way down in the last apartment, cross-legged, petting his dog. I know it's my buddy because I recognize his back and had known him for ten years. I sat there and watched him pet his dog for seven or eight seconds or whatever time it took me to walk from the front of the building back to where he was sitting. When I got to within maybe two feet of him, I knocked on the wall and made a noise; I didn't want to startle him or scare him in any way. At that point, the spirit entity of my buddy disappeared. He was 100 percent gone, but the dog didn't move. The dog just stayed there like nothing was happening. The kicker of the story and the most important part of this event was that the very next day, the dog was killed. He was run over by a truck, five feet from where I saw him!

UVX

One near-miss story happened in front of the UVX apartments sometime in the 1940s. A semitruck full of dynamite had pulled over in front of the apartments. The driver jumped out to run down to the English Kitchen for some coffee, not noticing that the brakes had started a fire in the back of the rig. A telephone operator was outside taking a break and saw the fire. The operator went to work and notified the fire department and the police chief, Tom Cantrell. They somehow put the fire out and stopped a very serious explosion. People in the apartments were evacuated. The telephone operator was rewarded, and the fire department and the police chief were celebrated. An explosion that could have leveled the Main Street and created many stuck spirits was prevented.

One fortunate day, I had a chance meeting with Deborah at Paul and Jerry's Saloon. Paul and Jerry's doubles as one of the town's great meeting places for social celebrations. It's the oldest saloon in Jerome (and possibly the oldest family-owned one in all of Arizona). It even had a bowling alley in its basement in the old days. The occasion was a baby shower, and Deborah just happened to sit next to me and shared some excellent spirit experiences. The first one occurred at the UVX apartments in unit C5.

Deborah had the day off and spent it lounging on the couch with her boyfriend, Jimmy. The couch abutted the doorway to the small kitchen. The only time she got up from the couch was to go to the bathroom. A friend of theirs came over that night with a twelve-pack, so she got up to put it in the fridge. When she walked into the kitchen, she noticed that the refrigerator had been moved. Neither she nor Jimmy had touched it, but it was two and a half feet from the wall.

"Jimmy pushed the refrigerator back, and it made the most godawful squealing noise," said Deborah. "There is no way it could have moved by itself." Their friend Melissa came to visit and said, "Oh, bad vibe in here…I am getting a father and son who had a fire in this apartment."

Shortly after this experience, Deborah met up with a friend who used to live in town. She asked Deborah where she was living. When Deborah told her the UVX in C5, her friend asked if she ever had anything odd happen

The United Verde Extension (UVX) apartment complex in the background, site of numerous hauntings. *Courtesy Jerome Historical Society.*

with appliances. She had lived in that apartment as well. She told Deborah that the gas stove used to turn on by itself in the middle of the night, and all of the hauntings were appliance related—all kitchen stuff. Perhaps the fire Melissa sensed happened in the kitchen.

Melissa related a similar UVX experience:

In 2004, we got an apartment in the UVX. I was only going to stay a couple of months. My apartment was clear, and a girl moved in down the way, into apartment 5. I came home from work one day, and she was standing outside the building. We became best friends. About six months later, in the winter, my friend kept waking up with her stove on. I told her to get me the next time it happened.

So she comes and gets me one night, and just as I'm leaving my apartment and walking toward hers, I hear this incredible screaming. She can't hear it. It's two older gentlemen and a boy, maybe fourteen years old, and they are up in the corner above the stove and they are kind of dirty. You can tell they are miners or lower class. I asked if I could help them. They said they wanted revenge against the man who set their house on fire—they died in the fire. It was why they kept turning on the stove. I assured them it was a long time ago and there was nobody to get revenge on.

I told them, "I can't help you in that way, but what I would like to talk about is you going home, crossing over, and going back to heaven. It will be much better than this entrapment bubble you have yourself in, the revenge and the vibration." They were having none of that. I could tell the boy wanted to go, but the two gentlemen didn't.

I talked to them a second time when it happened, and I said, "This is not OK. This is my friend's apartment, it is not yours, and if you don't want to move on that is your prerogative, but you can't continue to disturb her life like this."

One of my guides communicated to me at the time that spirits can only come through a portal for three weeks every year. It must be about the time that they died so every year they can reemerge in that time loop. So I told my friend to be patient, it will all be over in another week and that she could sleep in my apartment until it's over.

As mentioned earlier, Jerome has experienced its share of fires over the years, virtually burning down several times. It is possible that these spirits were seeking revenge for one or more of those fires.

Montana Hotel

Also on Company Hill was the elegant Montana Hotel, built by Senator Clark in 1900. This stunning hotel was meant to house one thousand miners until it burned to the ground in February 1915. Unfortunately, the prominent hotel, the envy of all the mining camps, was a total loss. Stories of residual hauntings in this area come from the miners who walked these stairways and boardwalks. Patricia was once pushed on a stairway in this area when no one was around.

Ellen experienced another spirit on Company Hill near the ruins of the Montana Hotel. She was alone at her friend Sherry's house, sleeping in the bedroom farthest from the kitchen, when she woke up to the sound of someone running around in the kitchen, dining room, living room and then Sherry's bedroom—and then slid right into bed with Ellen! Her heart was pounding; she was petrified. Running out to the street and yelling "Ghost!" didn't seem like the best option. She pretended to go to sleep, which she

The Montana Hotel loomed over town. It was the largest building ever built in Jerome, surrounded by Company Hill houses. *Courtesy Jerome Historical Society.*

eventually did. Ellen remembered hearing a whoosh of air as the male spirit hit the bedsheets.

Before we leave Company Hill, we have one more spirit experience that fits in well here, one that esteemed retired fireman Bill shared with us. He had just finished breakfast with our beloved fire chief, Rusty. Rusty had to drive back to the fire station for a minute. While Bill stayed in the car, he noticed what looked like the spirit of a man walking past the propane tank. The spirit looked like he was headed toward County Road, just below Company Hill. As the man moved past a clump of trees, he startled the birds and then disappeared. Bill said the spirit was visible for eight to ten seconds.

IN THE 'HOOD PLUS

THE "MARSHAL'S OFFICE"

On Main Street is an old but beautifully restored building referred to as the "Marshal's Office." Jessica, a past employee of the Jerome Historical Society and on-call nurse for our volunteer fire department, as well as a former tenant of this old Jerome building, imparted her otherworldly encounters:

I had decided to rent an apartment in Jerome, and when I was telling my friends about it, they cautioned me that previous tenants had moved out because of their experiences there. It was a woman and her lover, and he became unstable and impulsive, and verbally and emotionally aggressive. One day, he ran from that apartment down to Clarkdale. Just bizarre, impulsive and extreme behavior. They broke their lease and left early. I thought, "Well, I am a bright and shining light. I am good, and I will be OK." It didn't scare me. It didn't bother me.

The theory I have developed, being a woman of science but also a believer, is that the electromagnetic field of our dimension is how they can access us. My iPod would automatically fast forward when playing through the speakers. It would "dysregulate" somehow. I would hear my stainless steel teakettle scooch along the stove top. I would hear that from the other room, and it was always just playful and fun. I would say, "OK, I know you are in there, I see you." I was working in Sedona at the time and had contact with a reiki master, and she tuned into my space and told me that the energy there would like some cut flowers. The energy was dense. So I would bring home fresh-cut flowers. I honored the spirits, and I would play the music of that era.

Jessica noticed that whenever a gentleman friend of hers was in the apartment, he would become inconsiderate and verbally aggressive—not himself at all. Odd coincidence considering what had happened with the previous tenants.

Around this time, Jessica had gone through a tragedy at work and was processing it with her two best friends; her male friend was also present. He was so insensitive and cruel in his responses to the tragedy that Jessica got up and left the room. When she returned, her friend was in tears and realized that he had been brutal with her; he apologized, and they reached a level of clarity with what had happened.

Jessica has a sense that the spirits don't want another electromagnetic field around. They want their own space, so Jessica gives it to them. In the Marshal's Office, she gave them a room furnished with just a couch, a cedar chest and a dresser. Curiously, a black widow, also solitary creatures, set up shop right in the middle of the room, where a shaft of light lit it up.

Another time, Jessica had a more tactile experience with the spirits, which decided to play with her headphones. As she was relaxing to the music streaming into her ears, the volume kept increasing—certainly not a malfunction or an element of what she was listening to, said Jessica, nor was it the device itself. It would require a deliberate physical movement to turn up the volume on her headphones. She would turn the volume back down, but somehow the volume would go up again, as if someone was slowly dragging the volume lever up.

Jessica once made the mistake of accusing the spirits of stealing her favorite pair of earrings. She couldn't find them and said out loud in an accusatory nature, "Those punks!" Soon after, she noticed she had destabilized herself and was becoming less lighthearted. She began to avoid the use of alcohol and spent less time in her apartment, purposely staying outside more. She felt an uneasiness, and her relationships with her friends started to suffer.

"I was turning into an asshole and not an amazing version of myself," Jessica said with great self-clarity. At some point, she had an epiphany as she watched the situation unfold. One day, she returned home from a typically stable shift at work to pick up a few things and leave again. The moment she reached her floor of the building, she felt a sudden clutching around her solar plexus, her power center. It felt like something was grabbing and squeezing her, energetically and psychically. Jessica was convinced at that moment that the space had something to do with it. She never saw anything strange, but she certainly sensed strange energy. Even the private space she had created for the spirits wasn't enough.

Jessica moved away from Jerome after that, but not for long. She returned with the realization that if she was psychically strong, she would be less vulnerable to whatever was going on. Although she didn't feel there were ominous intentions with the energy, she believes that she may have been called to Jerome because of her empathic and intuitive nature, which lends itself to open and emotional situations "where people and spirits can dump their sadness on you," said Jessica. She believes that the spirits appreciate this aspect of her physical being.

The experience she had in her current residence involved a whirlwind romance around Christmas of the past year. When she realized it was not going to be much more than that, she broke it off, only to get a text message from her landlord days later telling her that this man had been in her house. He was no longer welcome there, and she didn't know he was coming over. She asked her landlord to look in and see if anything was destroyed or broken. He looked through her entire place and assessed that everything looked to be in order.

When Jessica got home, she went to the bedroom and immediately noticed that one of the three paintings hanging above her dresser had been moved. They were all portraits of her. The furthest one from the door was no longer on the wall but facedown on the other side of the dresser, placed in odd alignment with the dresser and the wall. It was not possible for the painting to have fallen in that way on its own. There was no explanation for it.

In the end, Jessica did find out that the whirlwind beau had taken a few of her things. She believes it was the spirits warning her that he was in the space by moving her painting. They had also tried to warn her he was trouble *before* she cut things off with him. In the midst of the romance, Jessica noticed one day that the lever for hot water at the kitchen sink faucet had been switched—she had to turn it to the off position to turn it on. Even the landlord couldn't account for it and also thought it was a little bit strange. Jessica believes that these oddities were the spirits warning her about "the dude rolling into her apartment without good intentions!"

Talking about Jerome spirits is something that Jessica is careful about. The men who worked the mines led an incredibly tortured life, and when they died so suddenly, they didn't get the chance to right the wrongs. She believes that these victim spirits are stuck, wanting to fix what happened to them—

they're not done. "These sudden deaths cause the spirits to linger because they didn't get a proper chariot to return them to the collective soul," said Jessica. The spirits Jessica encountered never felt like a personality—that there was much humanness associated with them—especially at the Marshal's Office. Instead, they were tortured souls, some ominous darkness, likely miners.

I mentioned to Jessica that I get goosebumps when I hear these stories. Jessica responded, "Yes, that is because our nervous system is an electromagnetic impulse, same with the heart. We are an electromagnetic field in ourselves, and that is how the spirits can access us."

Jessica is a spiritual woman. She wasn't a big believer in spirits before she came to Jerome. After experiencing it herself and witnessing the spirits accessing our dimension, Jessica now feels grateful to be able to help the spirits to have the experiences they need. She treats them with a lot of respect. Jessica believes that the spirits have an agenda that they seek to fulfill. That was part of her rationale for agreeing to this interview. Jessica knew that she could tell the story in a rational and nonjudgmental manner.

Simone's Home

Our anonymous waitress from the Grand Hotel, "Simone," told us about a spirit experience that happened when she moved into her new home:

When I first moved into my house, which was built in 1904, I would hear footsteps in my upstairs at about three in the morning. It sounded like someone wearing cowboy boots. I went up to make sure it wasn't an animal stuck or a squatter hanging out, and there was nothing. It freaked me out. I said out loud, "If you are here, I don't mind, but please don't interrupt or wake me up and don't bother me. I don't mind if you are here, but please don't make it so obvious." I would say it more in my head because I thought the spirits could read my mind: "You can be here, but please don't bother me. Please don't mess with me. I don't mind. I don't want to know that you are here." My neighbor said she could see the spirit of a man in the upstairs window of my house. Later, I had an intuitive male friend stay up there for almost a month who told me there was a spirit of male energy up there!

What Jerome looked like in the 1970s. The doors, windows and plumbing were taken for salvage. "Got to Rot Realty." *Copyright Michael Thompson.*

SALLY'S HOME

A very curious experience happened to Sally, another longtime resident and well-loved bassist and vocalist (and what a joy to hear her sing!):

One night when I was falling asleep, I heard a noise on the stairs. The stairs were just outside the bedroom. I closed my eyes when all of a sudden I felt something next to me. I opened my eyes, and there was a figure standing right there, really tall, maybe six-foot-two or so, looking down at me with his head tilted, right next to my bed. He had clothing on that was so bizarre. It appeared to be silk and shredded in little squares. It was so strange that I almost cannot explain it—almost like prayer flags but shredded on the ends. The material was grayish silver, and it covered his body. I couldn't quite see his face except for the eyes. However, the whole thing was made of shredded little tiny squares from head to toe, and it was blowing as though there was wind in the room. I thought I was dreaming so I shut my eyes, and I opened them again, and he was still there, and I did it again, and he was still there. The spirit entity wasn't doing anything except standing there, his head tilted, looking down at me.

I finally asked, "What do you want? What do you want?" I kept saying that, and he did nothing. Just these things blowing and fluttering and stuff on his shirt. Around the fourth or fifth time that I closed my eyes and opened them, he was gone. It was so crazy because, in the end, it was not negative. I wasn't scared to death. I was scared, but in retrospect, as I remember it now, I feel like I saw a kind soul, like someone looking down on me, kindly, benevolent. Because my dad had run away from home and I hadn't seen him in thirty-six years, I thought maybe he had died and came to visit me. Then I found my dad about a year later, so that wasn't it.

I have thought of it since then, and I believe the spirit is in the house. I don't seek it out or any of that. I feel almost like he is my protector in a way. I feel that way because it was so sweet in the end. There was no negative. It's a short little story, but honestly, I love it, I feel like it was a small gift to me. When this thing happened to me, I got less scared. When he didn't go away, I became less frightened. He was looking down with sweetness, and adoring, like "I am here to protect you."

FIFTH STREET

Melissa has lived and worked in several areas of town. She told of another spirit experience she had when she and her roommate moved to a house on Fifth Street:

There was a Hispanic spirit who just loved my friend, would follow her around everywhere. I told the spirit I could help her get unstuck from her situation, but she didn't care. Occasionally, she would glance my way, but it was like she was looking right through me. She couldn't see that I could see her. Everything is vibration. I couldn't tell my friend because she was completely freaked out by spirits and ghosts. Then one day, she was in the kitchen alone, and the spirit decided to play with her and tease her hair out. My friend turned around to see her hair falling to the ground. When I arrived home, she was out on the porch chain-smoking and asked me if there was somebody in there that I hadn't told her about. So I told her the whole story, that there was a spirit who was so enamored with her that she followed her everywhere and even watched her sleep. My roommate was upset with this news. The last time I saw that spirit I told her it was time for her to go home.

RON AND RUTHIE'S HOME

Ron and Ruthie built their house on land that had never been developed before. The land was previously the preliminary junkyard near the dump just outside town, so they had to haul away all kinds of garbage that had collected there.

They woke up one night, startled. They had been living in their brand-new house for about six months, even though it was not quite finished. At the foot of the bed was an interior wall. Ron opened his eyes and saw what looked like a casement window that swung into the bedroom, and an apparition of a little girl with dark eyes was staring at him from about ten feet away. She was looking right at Ron and reaching down to the desk, grabbing sheets of paper and stuffing them into her mouth. Ron was afraid to move. The spirit of the girl finally faded away. Ron's heart was racing, but he eventually fell back to sleep.

Ron and Ruthie believe that their pet chihuahua must have seen or felt this little girl spirit as well—it would go right to the landing by the interior wall and bark incessantly at the corner, right where the little girl was leaning through the casement window that wasn't there.

Several months later, this same apparition visited again. Even Ruthie's daughter saw her crossing the hallway late one night when she was watching television. Coincidentally, Ruthie's mother had read an article about the old days in the *Verde Independent* newspaper about a fatal horse-and-buggy accident that had happened in their area of Jerome. She called Ruthie—she had found out who their little spirit girl was.

"Sure as shit," said Ruthie, "it was about the surgeon who had worked for the mine. He and his little girl had gone down to Clarkdale to the pumpkin patch when it was close to Halloween and when they were driving back with a load of pumpkins, they hit a rut on the dirt road just as they were entering town. When they hit the rut, the little girl bounced out, and the wagon rolled over the young girl, and she died."

This accident happened near Ron and Ruthie's property. Ruthie's mother-in-law, who believed in the supernatural and had strong extrasensory perception, spoke with Ruthie about psychics and people who talk to spirits and how it was possible to send them away. Ruthie wanted to get rid of the little spirit girl because her grandsons were scared to go upstairs or sleep by themselves when they would come to visit; they had heard the adults talking about the little girl spirit. What did Ruth have to lose?

I just called to the little girl. I went to the corner where the dog was barking in the middle of the day, and I said, "Honey, I know what happened and that you are looking for your pumpkin. I know it was close to Halloween....I am so sorry you weren't able to go onto the other side. However, I have to ask you to leave because you are scaring my grandchildren."

I had gone to the store and bought the spirit girl a pumpkin. I took it to the corner where the dog had been barking and told her, "We are going to go out to the cemetery (we lived close to the cemetery), and we are going to fix the pumpkin up for you so you can have your pumpkin." I drew a face on it and said to her, "This way you can celebrate Halloween...and please don't come back. You can go ahead to the other side."

Ruthie said the spirit girl never did come back. After that, Ruthie believes that spirits could be asked to leave and that burning sage or incense around the house helped too.

Ron and Ruthie's family had an experience with a couple of spirits a few years later. Their son and grandsons, eight and thirteen years old at the time, were upstairs playing when they heard small voices, children's voices. Out of nowhere, two young boys made a ghostly appearance! This scared the living daylights out of the children, who immediately ran downstairs. Ruthie's son didn't know what to make of it. Her younger grandson was so scared he didn't want to go back upstairs again.

No one but her grandsons ever saw the boy ghosts. Ruthie believes that they may have lived in the area and perhaps just wanted to play.

Ruthie talked to her grandsons about the spirits and told them that she would ask them to leave. She convinced them to go upstairs with her so they could witness her doing this. Reluctantly, they did. They stopped at the top of the stairs, hesitant to go any farther, when the boy spirits suddenly came out of Ruthie's upstairs office—she couldn't see them, but she knew from her grandsons' faces that they were there. They started walking down the hall toward them. Ruthie's grandsons clutched onto her, petrified. The spirits stopped a few feet away from them and stood there for only seconds, looking at the two earthling boys, and then faded away.

After calming down her grandsons and hearing them out, Ruthie went into the office, opened up the door to the balcony and said out loud, "Boys, you guys gotta go. I am so sorry, and I don't know what happened or why you are here, and maybe you just wanted to play, but you're scaring my grandsons. Please go."

They must have complied because her grandsons never saw them again. As others have stated, Ruthie firmly believes that most spirits are not evil. They are benevolent, and there is a reason they are here.

After these experiences, Ron's take on spiritual entities has changed. "Now I legitimately and absolutely believe."

GOLD KING MINE

Melissa and her husband moved out to the Gold King Mine, at one point a ghost town and museum of sorts, just outside Jerome. It wasn't long before they were visited:

> One morning my husband is sleeping, and I wake up and see this little spirit boy sitting on the side of the bed next to him, tossing a ball up in the air. The boy said, "Time's a wastin'!" I didn't know it, but my husband had made plans to go fishing early that morning but had slept in. I guess the boy was going with him!

There were spirits all over the place out there. I have lived all over the U.S. and the Caribbean, and this is the second-most haunted place I have ever lived.

Melissa and her husband had been living out at Gold King Mine for two years when they discovered a very disturbing presence in their home. There was a step up from the kitchen to the living room, and at the step up, Melissa saw several spirit bodies lying on the floor in the fetal position, each missing one shoe. They all had similar skin tone and long, straight, dark hair. The spirit bodies started chanting, "We're here, we're here, we're here."

Melissa spoke to the spirit bodies, let them know that she could hear them and offered help. "They just wanted to tell me they were happy." She asked them what was going on and if they wanted to cross over, but there was no response. The chanting continued for months.

A few years went by before Melissa's neighbor, who worked in the Gold King Mine gift shop, called her one day. Two Native American ladies were at the shop and wanted to walk up the driveway toward Melissa's house—they had ancestors buried there who had been calling out to them. Her neighbor told the ladies the story of the spirit bodies Melissa had seen. They walked to the retaining wall by Melissa's house, looked around and left. They came back a week later with their ceremonial tools and released the spirit bodies.

PHELPS DODGE OFFICE

Jerome is a testament to very rough pioneer living and tough men and women who built a town on the side of a mountain on the edge of civilization. There were wonderful times as well as grim times. The mines closed several times for short periods. Belts were tightened, but the people made it through together.

Then, in 1938, Douglas shut down his Little Daisy operation. Only one mine remained. After a few years, Jerome lay in ruins and became a bona fide ghost town, the largest in the West.

Phelps Dodge had bought Clark's United Verde mining company in 1935 and left a well-loved and respected man in charge of the company property when the mine shut down in 1953. His name was John McMillan.

John was raised in Jerome and loved the town fiercely. He was one of the founders of the historical society and was also a pilot. He looked at his deserted, beloved Jerome and decided to reseed the town with vegetation. The mining and smelter activity had killed virtually every plant, which caused a major erosion problem during the summer monsoons. He seeded the town with very prolific Ailanthus trees, also known as the tree of heaven. This added life back to the tiny town.

The Jerome Historical Society was responsible for saving many of the buildings as well as the town. When the mining company was selling off the beautiful buildings for salvage, the newly formed historical society raised as much money as it could, bought a least a dozen buildings and saved what was left of the town.

A longtime Phelps Dodge employee, a respected resident of Jerome and former miner who knew the mines inside and out, kindly shared the following stories. The first one was told to him by Walter, another beloved Jerome resident and Renaissance man who passed away in 2017. I met the former miner in the old Phelps Dodge office building, where this first encounter happened with Walter while he was redoing the office floors:

> *Walter was standing in this room in the old office building. He said he felt like someone was looking at him, and when he turned around, the spirit of a Chinese man was right here in the doorway. Walter said that when you redo an old house, the spirits get upset about it—it stirs them up. We think the spirit was of the Chinese gentleman who is on a plaque we found in the basement. He was the caretaker of this building and died. Walter saw the same spirit there twice. The first time it happened, I was out in the field when Walter called and said he was at the bar. I said to Walter, "Isn't it a little early to be at the bar?" Walter replied, "Nope! I saw a ghost!"*

The former miner's daughter was about five years old when she encountered her first spirit at the old office building. She was standing on the chair next to the copier in the adjoining room. She jumped down and ran into her father's office to tell him there was a man who wanted to see him in the other room. There was a monitor on the door, so no one could enter without the staff being aware. The former miner went and checked the door, and it was still locked! He asked his daughter what the spirit said. She said he didn't say anything, but she knew he wanted to talk with him.

The last Phelps Dodge story happened to our storyteller's boss. He was down in Clarkdale, and his boss was in Jerome:

Phelps Dodge office building. Note the old train tracks out front. *Courtesy Jerome Historical Society.*

A current photograph of the old Phelps Dodge office building, site of numerous residual hauntings. *Copyright Michael Thompson.*

My boss tells me he has a pretty important conference call and asks if he could borrow the keys to the office and take the call there. I give him the keys and head down the mountain. When I get back up to Jerome, I see my boss is over in the parking lot. I grew up with his guy, mined with him for years, and know he is a solid dude, just like Walter was a solid dude. My boss told me that when he walked in the door of the old Phelps Dodge building, the ghost was standing at the bottom of the stairs looking at him. It was the same short Chinese dude that Walter had seen!

I'VE GOT A HAMMER

THE HAUNTED HAMBURGER
ON CLARK STREET

T he Haunted Hamburger restaurant is in a building originally established as a boardinghouse for miners of the United Verde Mining Company. The Haunted Hamburger recently expanded to the building next door, which was originally a telephone and telegraph office. The buildings are currently owned, and were well restored and repurposed by, Michelle and Eric Jurisin.

SPIRITS

For some background on the Haunted Hamburger building and name, the following information came directly from its website:

> *It all started years ago when Michelle and Eric Jurisin acquired the restaurant. The building, old and abandoned, was in need of great repair before it could be opened.... This is when the funny business began. As with all old buildings, when inhabitants take initial occupation, from its walls come the spirits to observe, and sometimes greet the newcomers. The Haunted Hamburger spirits were no different. Not only were these spirits curious but possibly frustrated tradesmen from long ago as it was tools that these spirits liked to take. More specifically, hammers. Yes, hammers. One hammer, then two, then three hammers had disappeared. Was this a case*

The Haunted Hamburger restaurant. This former rooming house and telephone/telegraph company building was repurposed as a popular restaurant. *Copyright Michael Thompson.*

of memory loss? At first, it was thought so until a prior owner asked the Jurisins if they had met the ghosts yet and to beware…they liked hammers! Shortly after this confirmation, the hammers began to reappear showing up in the most conspicuous places.

What followed next was literally too "in your face" to ignore, says Eric. One day, in the middle of repairs, he remembered he needed to go upstairs to finish a project. Just as he reached the top floor a door that he was standing next to slammed, nearly smashing him in the face. You could argue a cross breeze is strong enough to slam a door, and that would be true. Except, Eric had just sealed up all of the building's windows with thick plastic and tape to keep the cold winter air out. He knew there was no air current in the house.

What other odd occurrences frightened staff, owners and guests alike in the Haunted Hamburger? Cans flying off shelves, the hot water being turned on in the middle of the night. Distinct smells in the stairwell and even photographs guests have taken capturing the vague image of a woman.

This phantom woman has made enough appearances that she's been named Claire. She prefers to stay in the upstairs dining room next to the kitchen, where she's been known to tease the kitchen staff after an evening shift.

A HAPPY ENDING

THE CRIBS AND BORDELLOS

Jerome was a frontier town on the edge of civilization. In the 1880s, it was hardly civilized. Plenty of rough men drifted through Jerome for the copper mining work and formed the majority of the population.

In its heyday, Jerome had more than eight full-time bordellos and more than twenty saloons. The men needed ways to decompress after a hard shift at the mine. Most of the bordellos were in an area of town called the "Tenderloin District," behind the saloons on Main Street. A plaque marks "Husbands' Alley," a narrow passage to the cribs and bordellos the men could access after a bit of gambling and a few drinks at the saloon.

It is said that women were the civilizers of the wild western towns. In his book *Ghosts of Cleopatra Hill*, Herbert Young stated, "Although women were not allowed to work in the underground mines, their economic and social role was significant. They took care of homes and families and worked to support industries. They have always been central to Jerome's well-being." Young neglected to mention the numerous cathouses, cribs, brothels and bordellos and the valuable benefit they filled. The vestiges of Husbands' Alley and the Tenderloin District still exist in the heart of Jerome.

On the website Only in Your State, writer Monica Spencer noted this about prostitution in Jerome:

> *Sex work operated on a hierarchical scale. At the high end of the scale were classy ladies who worked in brothels operated by Madams who had a pretty cushy job. They often only provided (expensive) companionship for lonely*

men living in a town almost devoid of women.....At the low end of the scale were women working in the cribs, who somehow managed to see 30 to 80 clients per day. It was a rough job that had no guarantees or safety, and many women who worked the industry succumbed to the illnesses or violence associated with the job.

There are many stories about the horrors these sex workers endured, and history just barely remembers a few who died at the hands of their clients.

Prostitution started right on Main Street in the early 1880s. The first madam to open a "ladies' boardinghouse" was Nora Butter Brown. Ladies were few, and Nora did an amazing business and was known throughout the area.

Wyatt Earp and Billy the Kid even knew about her. One story goes that they were both at Nora's place at the same time, and Billy wanted to have a shootout with Wyatt. The shootout fortunately didn't happen due to some shenanigans Billy was up to, but Nora wrote that she was grateful to enjoy the pleasure of Wyatt's company. Wyatt was apparently in Jerome looking to buy a wagon to move his brother from Prescott to Tombstone, and Billy the Kid was stealing horses.

Jennie Bauters was Nora's protégé and known as "Belgian Jennie." She took over the boardinghouse when Nora Butter Brown moved to California in the late 1890s. Business was booming for Belgian Jennie, and she quickly became the richest woman in town. Her brothels weathered the fires of the 1890s, 1897, 1898 and 1899.

The building shown in the famous photograph here burned in the fire of 1898. Jennie ran into the street, promising favors for life if they could save her building. All was lost in a previous fire but rebuilt the next year. Jennie was smart enough to purchase insurance from Sanborn, and she soon opened another brothel in the Clinkscales building a little farther down Main Street.

Unfortunately, Jennie had her share of troubles between the fires, the law and the deaths and illnesses of her girls. In her book *Are Ghosts Real?*, Peggy Hicks tallied some of these troubles:

On January 9, 1900, Jennie had to appear in court with several of her girls as witnesses to a robbery that involved three railroad workers.

The following month, Jennie testified in the investigation of one of her girls named Rose Ames, who had died of an opium (laudanum) overdose.

One of Jennie's working girls died of a gunshot wound inflicted by Francisco Paca, a rejected suitor.

Another girl named Miss Fannie May contracted syphilis.

Jennie Bauters and her cathouse in 1898. Jennie was at one time the richest woman in Arizona. *Courtesy Jerome Historical Society.*

Jennie was expanding her brothel empire in 1905 when she was brutally murdered. She had gone to a developing gold strike in Mohave County near Kingman to a town called Gold Road. Jennie was in the process of setting up a bordello when her opium-crazed lover shot her in the back right on the street. He then riddled her dead body with five more shots. Then he shot himself but missed, merely wounding himself. He was hanged a few weeks later. Jennie is buried at Gold Road and was reputed to be the richest woman in the Arizona Territory at the time of her death.

Jennie's son took over the business and sold the building to John M. Sullivan, who converted it into a hotel. Later, cribs were added to the back of the Sullivan Hotel. The building still stands on Main Street and is the home of the popular Nellie Bly kaleidoscope shop.

An ordinance was soon passed that stipulated that brothels had to be located off of Main Street. Jerome was still a town with 90 percent men, so the brothels were merely moved to Hull Avenue, just below Main Street, near a notorious bar called the Wigwam, right across the street from the cribs. It was a very rough, violent area. A drunken brawl in the Wigwam in 1909 ended with nine men stabbed and cut by a knife. Law officers King and Hawkins had to break it up and arrested two of the men. All recovered from their wounds.

It wasn't long before Jerome appointed a brothel inspector. The ladies had to buy a tax license, and the working women had to register with the town and have an exam every two weeks.

Things were in order when the Cuban Queen came to Jerome in 1921. She purchased land and built her boardinghouse on a street designated for bordellos, with madams all around her: Diamond Lil's, the Black Cat across the street with Madam Pearl and Madam Rose.

The Queen had many aliases, but her real name was Bessie Johnson. She was from New Orleans and African American. When she got to Jerome, she

Cuban Queen bordello, built in 1922. It originally included a dance hall where the famous Jelly Roll Morton played. *Copyright Ron Chilston.*

felt the need to change her name to Anita Gonzales, bleach her skin and straighten her hair to pass herself off as Mexican. The Queen's ex-husband, the famous Jelly Roll Morton, aka Ferdinand LaMothe, came to visit and played piano in the Queen's bordello for a short time. Although some sources question whether they were ever legally married, it was commonly known that Anita was the love of his life.

In 1924, things got dangerous. The Queen hosted a wedding where an altercation broke out between the bouncer and an intoxicated guest. This was during Prohibition, so the source of the man's intoxication was of interest. Of course, it was the Queen's establishment. Later, Francisco Villalpando was shot dead by Jose Rodriquez in the middle of the street.

In 1927, murder tainted the Cuban Queen's bordello. The unfortunate woman was named Guadalupe Villalpando, Francisco's wife and mother of five. She was allegedly fighting with a client named Pablino Jauriqui, who shot her in the head and then shot himself twice in the throat. Something was a bit strange about this murder. Hicks stated in *The Ghosts of the Cuban Queen* that the Queen and her new husband, Jack Ford, seemed to know more about it, but they would not tell. The Queen changed her story several times. This court trial put the Queen in the spotlight, and the newly formed branch of the KKK in nearby Prescott, Arizona, was watching. Jack soon heard that the Klan were coming for the Queen. She sold her place to a working woman she liked, the couple hastily packed up their car and off they went to Oregon and a new life. Right before they left, they took five-year-old Enrique with them, the youngest Villalpando child. The Queen and Jack raised him and named him Henry Ford. Henry didn't find out about this until he was an old man.

The 1930s were no better for the prostitutes. In 1931, a brutal murder occurred at Diamond Lil's, also known as Lil's Place. A working woman by the name of Sammie Dean was violently strangled. Sammie was beautiful and even had her own car. There were important men involved with this murder, and to this day, it has never been solved. One suspect was the mayor's son, who was in love with Sammie and asked her to marry him. She refused, and he vowed to get revenge. The mayor was *also* seeing Sammie, as was the sheriff's son. The police showed no interest in investigating this murder.

The Sammie Dean case is another example of how lax the law was back in the early days of Jerome. Roberto, who grew up in Jerome, moved away and became a criminal attorney and then returned to Jerome in his retirement, remarked about the trial, "The inquest was a sham and nobody

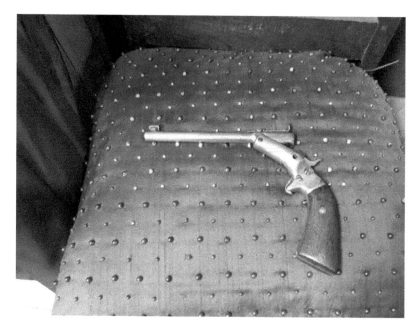

This J Stevens single-shot .22 "Tip-Up Pistol" with walnut grips was found in a Jerome home. It was quite popular with the ladies. *Courtesy Peggy Hicks.*

was ever prosecuted. At the inquest, a person was asked if they saw who did it and the response was 'Oh, everybody knows who did it.' The chief suspects were either of two guys: the son of the sheriff or the son of the mayor. The conclusion was 'homicide by persons unknown.' The inquest was held two hours after the body was discovered. That was Jerome."

Needless to say, this was a very dangerous part of Jerome in the 1930s. The Nevada Café, where Officer Rees was shot dead in 1933, was right across the street from the cribs. The murder of Officer Rees was never solved.

SPIRITS

Eventually, prostitution became illegal in Jerome. They say that the spirits of these women still walk the town, sometimes appearing near the quarters where they worked. Patricia has often commented that she believes the most haunted area of Jerome is in the Tenderloin District, behind the Sullivan building near the women's jail.

The old Cuban Queen Bordello sadly fell to ruin in a windstorm in March 2017. All that remains are rubble at the site and some photographs to show you what a queen she was. The original building was said to have a saloon and dance hall.

Renee stood in front of the Cuban Queen one day and could see the madams sitting at the kitchen table next to the stove, having tea. When she sees something like this, it doesn't mean she is seeing ghostly entities but rather the energetic imprint of something that happened in the past.

The Cuban Queen had just been surveyed when a local realtor named Peggy was checking the survey flags. All of a sudden, she felt weak in the knees and decided to sit down. Something caught her eye as she looked up. It was an image of a lady standing on a balcony—only the balcony had fallen down years ago and this lady spirit was hovering in midair.

The old Diamond Lil's is now private residences and an Airbnb site. I ran into the current owner, who coincidentally mentioned that a recent guest had had a spirit experience as I was working on this chapter. She had just checked in five minutes before when she felt a tap on her shoulder and heard a voice say "Hello." Nobody was in the apartment but her. She wondered whose spirit it was and hoped it was just letting her know it was there.

Deborah had her own spirit encounter at Diamond Lil's:

I lived in an apartment that Phil owned, behind La Victoria; I was on the top floor. It was my favorite apartment, and at the time I was seeing a man named Bob…he worked sporadically. We had windows within the apartment, and every now and again during the day I would see people go by the window and I would look up and think, "OK, I am just seeing things or maybe it was Bob, and I would say 'Bob?' and there was nobody there."

So then, one night, he was somewhere, and I had gone to bed early. I had a feeling somebody was looking at me. And I opened my eyes, and a man was standing by the bed. And he was wearing a morning coat and a top hat, and he had glasses and Van Dyke facial hair. So I said, "Hello, it's nice to meet you finally. Thank you for sharing your space." I blinked, and he had moved into the corner of the room, and I said again, "Thank you for sharing your space, it was nice to meet you and goodnight." I rolled over, and my heart was going VA VOOMP! VA VOOMP!!! I rolled back over and opened my eyes, and he was gone.

The next night, I was at Paul and Jerry's, and I was telling a friend what I had seen. Jay was the bartender, and he came in about halfway through the story. He walked down the bar and said, "Was this guy wearing…." He said exactly what the guy was wearing! I said, "Yes! Who is he?" It turned out below my apartment in Jay's apartment there

La Victoria Market serviced the bordello area—located next door to Diamond Lil's and across the street from the Black Cat bordello. *Copyright Ron Chilston.*

had been a decapitation. She [the victim] was a prostitute, and it had been a bordello back in the day. She was decapitated with a piano wire, and there were two suspects. One was the mayor and one was his father or son (I don't remember which). So Jay thinks this man was the father of the son. The theory was that the prostitute wanted to leave the life and get married to the father and that the son was in love with her and killed her. The father felt guilty, so that is why he still shows up.

Who was this spirit? Who were the ladies having tea? Who was the one tapping the guest on the shoulder and saying hello? There was no shortage of deaths and murders in this area. The spirits could be one of several past madams or soiled doves.

STILL HERE

THE CONNOR HOTEL AND SPIRIT ROOM BAR ON MAIN STREET

T he Connor Hotel has been lovingly restored and renovated by longtime Jerome resident and current owner Anne Conlin. We gathered some of the Connor Hotel's history from the Southwest Ghost Hunters Association:

> Built in 1898 by David Connor, the Connor Hotel has a colorful past, ranging from the heights of luxury to the depths of squalor and back again.... This first-class lodging establishment also offered a barroom, card rooms, and billiard tables on the first floor. Rooms were rented on the "European plan," for the princely sum of $1.00 per night. The stone foundations were quarried from the hills around Jerome, and the brick was fired in nearby Cottonwood.

SPIRITS

During her interview in May 2018, Mary, who works the Connor Hotel lobby, told us of an experience with a spirit and a camera:

> A woman came in and stood by the brick wall, then held up her camera and took a photo of herself. She walked right over to me to show me that the photograph also contained a Mexican-looking man, shorter than her and

Left: Connor Hotel. The Spirit Room was once a restaurant for the hotel. It is where Anna Hopkins threw the acid. *Copyright Michael Thompson.*

Below: Current photograph of the Connor Hotel. All twelve rooms have hauntings. It burned down and was rebuilt in 1898. *Copyright Ron Chilston.*

with a mustache. The interesting thing is that in that very space was a bar, and the bar owner fit the description of the man. His name was Kito. She was just a young woman who happened to choose that corner to take a selfie. There is a photograph of Kito in the Connor.

Sally, a local resident, told of a close and very credible friend who stayed at the Connor, and every time she would look into the mirror, she would see the spirit of a little girl run behind her. She saw her at least twice and never felt any fear about it.

One gruesome incident that happened at the Connor involved Anna Hopkins, the wife of the local mining company's chief engineer. As reported on the website Only in Your State, "Anna believed that her husband was in some relationship with a local schoolteacher and decided to enact revenge herself. In 1922, Hopkins threw carbolic acid into the face of the teacher in the downstairs café of the Connor Hotel."

There is another story that needs to be told here for the reader to get a sense of what Jerome was like at the time. This experience involved the daughter of the aforementioned Anna Hopkins and was relayed to me by Roberto:

Anna Hopkins's daughter got pregnant by a Mexican boy. This was something that was unheard of at the time, and the town wanted to lynch the boy. The sheriff put the boy in jail for protection, however, the townsfolk set the jail on fire. The sheriff then shot the boy to spare him from being burned to death. The child was born, and some of the ancestors of that child have come to Jerome to pay their respects.

Roberto relayed a similar story that also involved a young woman getting pregnant. This was a young Mexican woman who became pregnant by one of the town's bigwigs. They took her out to Hulls Canyon and pushed her over the edge. There was no investigation. That was the way things were handled back then sometimes.

Following is a verbatim interview with the delightful owner of the Connor Hotel, Anne Conlin. Her wording and descriptions are excellent. It is this author's hope that in reading Anne's words, the reader will get a sense of her supersweet and sincere being:

My dad and uncle bought the hotel back in 1980 when it was pretty derelict. The rooms were rented out through the bar, and therefore it was instead a flophouse. My dad and uncle did some horse trading, and my uncle wound up not being a co-owner. In 1999, my parents brought me on board to put some sweat equity into the situation, and we began renovating it and prepared to open it up again as a nice hotel rather than a pay-as-you-go flophouse through the bar. As our contractor, Harry, hauled out many years of the old furnishings, he and his partner said, "Oh, if these old mattresses could only speak!" To which I thought, "I am happy they can't." We reopened it in 2000, and it has been a lot of fun—a lot of guests, a great big learning curve along the way, and many ghost stories. Staff and guests have reported a lot of different spirit experiences. Unfortunately, I have never had a spirit experience, so whatever is going on is going on in a plane that I am not able to perceive, and for that, I am kind of grateful.

I do take the stories with some degree of a grain of salt because I know that many people do come to Jerome looking for spirits, and often you find what you are looking for. At the same time, when we hear the repetition of specific themes or experiences, it does make one pause and wonder and think, "That's curious." We have heard this before about room 5. So I certainly keep an open mind about the existence of certain supernatural goings-on. If I were a guessing person, I would say, "Yeah, there is more there than meets the eye, and who are we to pretend to know everything that is going on in this vast universe when we are such tiny little ciphers, each one of us. Is there more out there than we are perceiving? Well, I should imagine so.

Anne then proceeded to tell me one of several ghost stories, saying that it was a curious one:

It was probably about five or seven years ago when I had a lovely Belgian woman in my employ at the time. She was an elegant woman, and her name was Katrien. Katrien was a critical front desk employee of mine. She was working at the desk one busy Saturday afternoon when she received a complaint from some guests that there were loud, drunken and disruptive guests in room 6 and something needed to be done about this. Unfortunately, this sort of thing does on occasion happen in a hotel, and Katrien is a tiny little woman.... She announced that she would go upstairs and get the situation sorted out. My bar manager at the time was a lovely man named Chuck. Chuck happened to be in the lobby and heard this situation arising and very chivalrously said that he would go with her. He didn't think she should go up and confront drunken guests on her own. So Katrien and Chuck headed upstairs together and knocked on the door of room 6 sharply. The people came to the door, they talked, and it went relatively smoothly, and the situation seemed to be headed toward a peaceful resolution. When the door to room 6 closed, the door directly next to it, to room 5, began to shake violently in its frame. It was weird. They wondered, "What the hell is this?" Now Katrien and Chuck knock on the door of room 5 and get no answer. Katrien says, "Well this is weird," because she realizes she hadn't checked anybody into that room yet. To be safe, they head back downstairs and check the booking, and nobody had checked into that room. So up they go and knock again and no answer, open the door, and there is nobody there and no sign that anyone has been there. The room is tidy and made up and ready for a guest, but there is nobody there.

Anne commented that it is one thing to have one person invent something or misperceive something or have a little bit of a hallucination or whatever you might want to call that, but Chuck and Katrien *both* saw the same thing. She said that Chuck is the most settled and sensible sort of fellow that you would ever hope to meet. Curiously, those two rooms are right at the center point of the hotel, along with room 11, which is directly across the hall. Somehow those three rooms have been an odd nexus for some happenings.

Anne offered another story in which her young cousin Bobbie, who owns Bobby D's BBQ restaurant in town, had a weird experience also involving rooms 5 and 6:

He was staying in room 6 some years ago with his girlfriend. Bobbie thinks he must have walked in his sleep because he suddenly he found himself out in the hallway in his underwear. So he made haste to rush back into his room and jump back into bed and curl up next to his girlfriend. Unfortunately, he entered the wrong room, and the woman, who wasn't his girlfriend, screamed when she realized a strange man had just jumped into bed with her. It turned out that her husband had somehow found himself out in the hallway at the same time, and Bobbie had obviously rushed back into the wrong room. It was a weird tangle of coincidences. Bobbie felt like he had had an out-of-body experience, almost as if he had been momentarily possessed. He woke up from his sleepwalking when the woman screamed.

Anne went on to share an interesting aspect about that section of the hotel, as well as more peculiar incidents experienced by hotel staff:

It has a similar thread. Scary for the guests. This is minutia and maybe beside the point, but I will mention it as a sort of tie-in. Right at the center point in the hotel is a place where the hotel has settled apart over the last century and a quarter, to the extent that twenty or so years ago, Harry was summoned to come in and do severe bracing and support with I-beams to go all the way down to bedrock in the basement to stop the settling process. However, even now if you are at that point in the hallway, you can visually see that if a ball is dropped on either side of you, the ball would roll to each end of the hall. We kind of halted the settling process, but you can extrapolate or theorize that this is where the building has gapped to let in all of that energy, right around rooms 5, 6, and 11.

We had someone with supposedly psychic ability stay in the hotel at one point, and she reported that in her professional opinion (take this as you will) that there was a gap into another layer of being or a world or consciousness in that corner of the building, specifically in the closet of room 8. Call me silly, call me susceptible because I am, ever since then, I have been unsettled by that closet. Honestly, if I have had to go in there on my own, I haven't liked it. Moreover, my daughter Eva, who is my head of housekeeping and is a pretty hard-headed and sensible young woman, has reported also feeling very uneasy about room 8. Eva has also had more than one curious and unsettling experience in that room, such as things being moved; her little carrier of housecleaning supplies turning up inexplicably in a new location in the room. At one time when Eva was cleaning in the back of the hotel, cleaning supplies in hand as she was exiting room 8 to head over to room 7 to continue working, her broom handle clanged against her metal bucket. It gave that distinctive sound of something clanging on metal, and thirty or forty-five seconds later as she was going into room 7, which is maybe twenty-five feet down the hall, the clanging noise from back at room 8 exactly repeats. It was way too far out in time to be an echo.

Room 7 is another odd spot that Eva and Monica, who is now at my front desk, have separately and together have witnessed oddities. One curiosity is that room 7 seems to have a repeated pattern of the door being found ajar the next morning, even after it wasn't rented. The housekeeping staff has been positive about locking it up because that is the end of their routine every day. Monica worked housekeeping one winter day. She had locked everything up at the end of the day. When she came into work the next morning, she perceived that the door to room 7 was ajar. That was odd, and not for the first time either. Monica goes down the hall kind of in trepidation, wondering if someone is in there. When she opens the door, she finds that it's untouched and immaculate, but the little gas-fired, faux woodstove is blasting, and the room is ninety degrees! Monica, who is very detail oriented, undoubtedly did not leave the heat on in a room that was not booked for the night!

Anne shared a funny story that happened with one of her other staff members, "an interesting and classy lady" named Dinah who has been with Anne right since they reopened the Connor Hotel:

> *She comes to work with her long salt-and-pepper hair pinned up and wears an immaculate period dress. Her passion is roses, and she has hundreds at her home in Cottonwood. She cuts them and tries to keep fresh roses in each hotel room. In her usual attire, she is grungy and in dungarees, but she dresses the part for work. Dinah has said to me memorably that when she dresses for work, she feels like a longshoreman in drag—but she pulls it off well! She was in the front window once doing a display when a young boy walked by with his mother on Main Street. Dinah heard the boy say to his mother, "Momma, there's a ghost in there!" Dinah looks so classic in the period and attire, it's no wonder the boy thought she was a ghost. Dinah has kept a ghost log over the years in which she has people jot down their experiences.*
>
> *Is there something at the Connor? Yes, I have heard enough that I think I can say there is. Is it a deeply scary thing? No, I don't think so, because I can comfortably work upstairs alone. I might look over my shoulder a time or two, and there may be certain spots like that closet in room 8, but for the most part I feel comfortable and I am grateful for that. I don't want to feel afraid, especially somewhere where I essentially live all the time.*

Who are all the spirits at the Connor Hotel? David Connor? Anna Hopkins? Past miners? The possibilities are endless considering Jerome's history.

A very popular bar and music venue in Jerome is the Spirit Room, once the dining room for the Connor and right around the corner from what was known as the Tenderloin District in Jerome. This was the part of town where most of the prostitution ensued and where the women's jail was also located.

The story goes that one of the prosperous madams would take her ladies out for breakfast on Sunday mornings at the Connor dining room. They were always dressed to the hilt and had gobs of money—much to the dismay of the local churchgoers.

Now that it is a famous watering hole, several people have reported being touched by the spirits while sitting at the bar. Many photographs taken inside the Spirit Room show orbs floating in the frame, an alleged telltale sign of ethereal presence, and some tourists claim to have seen them bopping in videos taken

The Spirit Room bar, recently voted the best small-town bar in Arizona. A must stop on Halloween! *Copyright Michael Thompson.*

of the often crowded dancefloor. The Spirit Room and the Connor Hotel are teeming with spirits from the past.

Jane—one of our well-loved artists, a longtime resident and the former mayor—bartended at the Spirit Room in the early 1980s. She worked nights and has this spirit experience to share:

> *It had been a busy Saturday, and the bar was closing at one o'clock. It was between one and two in the morning, and I was the only one in the bar. I was cleaning up and making sure that everything was in order and had my back turned to the bar when I just caught an apparition of a person walking from the side door to the phonebooth. It looked like he or she had a long coat on—it was just a quick glimpse of a figure passing across the room. It didn't creep me out. It was just kind of an odd feeling. I didn't know if it was a man or a woman, but whoever it was had on either a long dress or a long coat, period clothing of the 1890s or 1900.*

Jane has never been afraid of ghosts or believed that they were real. She doesn't know what she saw, but she knows she saw something! Several other people in town have also reported seeing spirits cross the dance floor to the phone booth. There used to be a long line at the phone booth during the mining days. Could these be the spirits of miners trying to contact lost loved ones?

THE SHOW MUST GO ON

LIBERTY THEATRE ON JEROME AVENUE

Built where several saloons had burned down when Jerome was ravaged by fires in the late 1800s and early 1900s, the Liberty Theatre was completed in 1918, but it didn't open until 1919 because the town was under quarantine due to the Spanish influenza epidemic. The Liberty Theatre showed silent movies and had a stage for vaudeville and boxing events. It closed in 1929 because the owner didn't want to invest in sound equipment. The bottom floor was converted into a café for a short time, and its Robert Morton pipe organ was removed in 1965.

Only four proprietors have owned the theater. A man named Leo bought it in the 1960s and supposedly kept rattlesnakes in the basement—he occasionally let them out! The current owners are Bob and Debra Altherr; they bought the Liberty in 2003. Although the street level is now a gift shop, the theater is virtually intact and open to the public. They still have the original projection equipment in the theater booth.

SPIRITS

One story that has circulated about the Liberty Theatre building is that it is supposedly haunted by the ghost of a former patron. The woman immigrated to the United States from Germany and was involved in a passionate though tumultuous relationship with another immigrant that eventually ended in her death.

The Liberty Theatre, a silent movie theater, is on the right. You can see the eagle before it fell down. *Courtesy Jerome Historical Society.*

After a heated argument with her lover, the woman went to the Liberty to watch a film and calm down. Unbeknownst to her, he followed and sat behind her during the movie. Just as the organ music thundered through the theater to accompany a dramatic scene, he strangled her to death. The woman's ghost is said to haunt the upper floor of the theater.

Although this story is on the web and has been told around town, we have not found any documentation to validate it. Nothing is written about this murder in the cemetery or newspaper records that we could find. We wonder if it was just made up. Take it with a grain of salt.

While an Australian couple were on a ghost tour that stopped at the Liberty, the husband had an eerie encounter. They returned to the theater after their tour and asked to go back upstairs because he just "needed to go back." He was visibly shaken by what he experienced. Upstairs, he had been slapped in the face by a spirit so hard that he actually fell forward a bit. When he returned to the area where the slap happened, he experienced cold chills and then came back downstairs. The man told Debra that his wife was a believer but he was not—until he experienced the phantom slap in the theater.

If you look above the door on the front of the Liberty Theatre, you can see where a large concrete banner used to be attached to the building. Above the banner was a large cement eagle. In the 1980s, a woman who worked at the Liberty was able to communicate with a presence that told her the eagle was about to fall. The woman told the police and requested they cordon off the area—it was where the school bus would drop off the children in the afternoon. The police coned it off, and sure enough, the eagle fell that day. One of the schoolchildren, a grown Jerome woman today, brought a piece of the eagle to school for show and tell. Thank goodness for that presence alerting the shopkeeper and for the police responding!

On one occasion, Debra had a paranormal investigator take a tour upstairs to where all the musical instruments were kept. The instruments were not set up to be played, but out of nowhere, the drum started beating all by itself. The investigators also captured an image of a woman's profile in the projection window.

Debra shared several stories with me about customers who have had spirits show up in their photos. One lady who had taken a photograph ten years earlier came back to show Debra. In the background of the photograph were two men in long coats and hats with satchels over their shoulders. They were clearly in the photo, but nobody was upstairs in the theater when the lady took the snapshot. She was so curious about it that

Main Street after the fires of the 1890s and before Arizona prohibition in 1915. Note the bandstand and parade. *Courtesy Jerome Historical Society.*

she sent it to be analyzed to make sure that the image in the photo was accurate—and it was.

Another couple was filming upstairs in the theater, and when they got home they heard children's voices in the footage. The balcony was where the children would sit to watch movies.

Another person capturing video in the theater saw a ball of light float up out of one of the chairs. One paranormal investigator showed Debra a photograph she had taken of a ghost that appeared as a green line. The investigator said it was energy and that it was the best photograph she had ever taken. Another customer took a selfie with her phone, and in the photo was a person sitting next to her—in actuality, nobody was there.

Debra had another paranormal investigator tell her that he had seen the spirit of a young girl playing jacks. When he asked the spirit what she was doing, she said she was waiting for her father, who was changing the lamps and cleaning the chandeliers upstairs.

A woman was about to make a purchase one day, and before Debra was able to bag it up, the woman ran out of the store. Apparently, while she was paying for her merchandise a presence appeared next to her, and she just had to go! Debra says that she has many customers go upstairs and tell her they can feel the energy.

Who are all these spirits? Whose energy is it? Another visitor told Debra that she was seeing a bunch of tables with men playing cards and that a fight was happening. Could the spirits be men who died in the saloon fires before the Liberty was even there? So curious.

LET THE GOOD TIMES ROLL

SPOOK HALL ON HULL AVENUE

S pook Hall, as it's known by Jerome locals, was formally called Lawrence Memorial Hall in honor of Richard E. Lawrence, a significant contributor to the Jerome Historical Society and the first Jerome postmaster. The building was initially constructed for the Dicus Garage and gas station. It was later remodeled to house J.C. Penney after the building it was in was destroyed in a series of landslides in 1936. The department store reopened in 1937 at this location and closed in 1953.

Spook Hall is the town community center. Events of all kinds happen here, from the annual Halloween dance and Christmas potluck to weddings, memorials, art shows, conferences, humane society flea markets and family reunions. The venue is available to rent through the Jerome Historical Society.

The most anticipated event in Jerome is the annual Halloween masquerade dance. This awesome fundraiser organized by the Jerome Fire Department Auxiliary benefits the town's volunteer fire department. The party has been held for forty-four years and draws guests from all over the world. Returning revelers book their overnight accommodations a year in advance.

After the big slide on Main Street, J.C. Penney moved its store to Spook Hall in 1937. This is an area where there were many bordellos. *Courtesy of the Jerome Historical Society.*

Hull Street after the slide of 1936. The only surviving buildings were the Dicus Garage and Spook Hall (J.C. Penney). *Courtesy Jerome Historical Society.*

Dicus Garage repair shop and car dealership for Buick, Plymouth and Studebaker automobiles. It is Cody DeLong Studio today. *Courtesy Jerome Historical Society.*

SPIRITS

Spook Hall is on the site where many small shacks, also called cribs, were used by the "sporting ladies" to entertain their guests. One prostitute was stabbed to death by a miner in this location. Her spirit is what haunts the building. She is often seen in front of Spook Hall and then vanishes.

Patricia was leading a ghost tour in this part of town when the spirit of a huge man carrying a lunchbox appeared in the street just in front of Spook Hall. He was so real that she called out to him. He was dressed like a miner and wearing a helmet. Patricia saw the figure, a guest on her tour took a photo and got it and then the spirit disappeared! Perhaps this apparition was a miner who had just enjoyed a diversion from his hard labor, or maybe he was the murderer of the unfortunate prostitute, hoping to meet up with her in the next realm?

FIERCE PASSION

MILE HIGH GRILL AND INN ON MAIN STREET

The Mile High Grill and Inn, built in 1899 in one of Jerome's more prominent structures, was known as the Clinkscales Building. This building was erected directly on top of the ashes of the previous one and has walls eighteen inches thick to make it as fireproof as possible.

The current owner of this beautiful historic building is longtime beloved Jerome businesswoman Liz Gale. This awesome quote from the Mile High's website sums up Liz and the charm of this town: "Her passion...is Jerome....In all of its copper mining, ghost haunting, motorcycle riding, crazy, hippie, openly liberal, closeted republican, artist, intelligent, informed, dog loving, beer chugging, gay friendly, wine sipping, story-telling, book reading, the local drinking on the steps watching the tourists, you never know if you're talking to a bestselling author, rock star or guy living in a tent on the hill glory, she can't imagine being anywhere else."

This building housed the original bordello of the famous Madam Jennie Bauters. After a time, when Jerome became more "civilized," the bordellos were forced to move off Main Street to the Tenderloin District. Jennie was murdered and is believed to haunt this location.

Above: The Mile High Grill and Inn, originally a hardware store, then one of Jennie's bordellos and now a popular inn and restaurant. *Photo by Midge Steuber.*

Left: Ore wagon on Main Street, heading back to the mine. The TF Miller Building is in the distance. Living was rough. *Courtesy Jerome Historical Society.*

SPIRITS

Troy Taylor of American Hauntings Ink posted this online: "Jennie and her phantom cat have frequently been reported....The cat often vanishes before guests can pick her up and loves to brush against people in the kitchen. Jennie often moves things about in the kitchen as well and keeps the maid busy by rearranging furniture, moving objects and rotating the ceiling fan."

Another guest grabbed her phone to videotape the edge of the bed as something appeared to be walking across it, stopping and then sitting or lying on the bed, leaving the covers slightly disheveled. The nickname Sipps has been given to this ghostly cat.

Melissa has a few experiences to share from her days working at the Mile High:

So I am working as a housekeeper at the Mile High, and I have static cling on one side of my body. Joanne sees me pulling on my leg one day and she tells me that the cat got me. I ask her what she is talking about and she says there is a cat who belonged to a woman who lived up here and will rub on people's legs. I never saw the cat, but the evidence of this weird static cling would happen on one side of my body every day when I was cleaning. And when I am cleaning, I keep thinking that something is following me around. I don't see anyone, and I know this is a neat trick of a disembodied spirit.

Finally one day I bent down to put some sheets in the dryer, and when I come back up, a woman is standing there like this [puts her hands on her hips]. *She had on capri pants, a T-shirt and a pixie bob. She looks like she is from the 1960s. The manager I worked with, Juanita, used to always stand like that. I said, "Darn it, Juanita, you scared the shit out of me!" Then I realized it wasn't Juanita at all but the spirit who had been following me around. The spirit just smiled and disappeared, and I never saw her again.*

There was another spirit lady in an 1890s dress that appeared to Melissa when she was in the room with the log bed at the top of the stairs. This spirit used to love moving objects around. Melissa thought she was losing her mind because she knew she had placed an item in a specific place but it wouldn't be there the next time she looked. Nobody stayed there that night. One time, Melissa saw the spirit crossing the hallway, and she asked her what her fascination was with the object she kept moving. Melissa felt the spirit was angry and bitter. The final time Melissa encountered her she

Current photograph of the business district looking down Main Street. *Copyright Ron Chilston.*

Artist rendering, oil: *Sullivan Turns 100*. The tall building is Sullivan Apartments, next to Safeway Pay N Take it. Arizona Hotel is in the background. *Copyright Cody DeLong.*

was mopping one of the bathrooms, and the spirit yanked the mop out of Melissa's hands. Melissa turned around and told the spirit that she would not tolerate touching.

She said to the spirit, "If you want to talk about crossing over into heaven, I am here for you all day, but if you just want to pull your shenanigans and stay stuck where you are, then we have nothing to talk about. And you will not touch me again!"

Melissa believes that people don't realize they are in control in these unearthly encounters. Yes, they should be cautious, but they don't have to be afraid of spirits. If they clearly express their boundaries, the spirits won't cross them. Melissa cringes when hosts on the ghost shows say, "Touch me, show me you are real." She says this gives the spirits permission to contact you or enter you, and that's not what you want to do.

RIDE 'EM, COWBOY

GHOST CITY INN ON MAIN STREET

The beautiful Ghost City Inn was built in 1890 as a boardinghouse for the mine company's middle management team. Although most of its life has been spent as a boardinghouse, this Jerome building also served as an ashram as well as a restaurant in prior years. It's currently owned and lovingly cared for by Richard Faye and Ingrid Sarris.

SPIRITS

A cowboy shows up in the bathroom at about three o'clock in the afternoon to wash up from a shift and fills washbasins with soapy water. This appears to be a residual haunting at the inn that repeats itself. The cowboy is also known to return at about three o'clock in the morning to wash for the next shift.

The building is also known as the Garcia House for a family who owned it for more than fifty years. Grandma Garcia is said to have hated smoking. The story goes that during Prohibition, the Garcia men decided to set up a still and make their own liquor. Well, the still started a small fire right next to Grandma Garcia's room. Grandma Garcia was terrified of fire after that. Today, whenever someone smokes a cigarette or lights a candle, it makes the spirit of Grandma Garcia very nervous, so she appears and makes mischief.

Jackie, one of the previous owners, bought the inn in 2001 and had an average occupancy of 30 percent. There were days when she only had one

Current photograph of the popular Ghost City Inn, home to the residual cowboy haunting and Grandma Garcia. *Photo by Midge Steuber.*

room occupied. She remembered a couple in their seventies who stayed at the inn one time. The next morning, the lady guest said to Jackie, "Oh my goodness, I feel so sorry for you!" When Jackie asked her why, she replied, "You must not get any sleep at all." Jackie told the elderly couple that she is always asleep at nine o'clock. "But we heard you come back last night at 2:30 a.m. and check those people in," said the guest, confused, "and they walked and walked and walked and went up and down the stairs and didn't settle down for close to an hour." Jackie reassured her that everything was locked and they were the only guests. Quite puzzled, the old couple was sure they had heard people talking.

Grandma Garcia had the house back in the early 1900s and raised her granddaughter Oralee there until she was a teenager. Oralee visited Jackie and her husband when they owned the inn and shared a few interesting stories about the boardinghouse. She said that miners worked eight-hour shifts around the clock. They were getting ready for work at all hours, and Grandma Garcia cooked all their meals and packed their lunches. Jackie wondered why guests would report hearing conversations and movement around two o'clock in the morning if nobody else was there. Who would be walking around and making noise? The guests would even smell coffee and perfume. Apparently, there was a shift change at 2:30 a.m. Oralee also told Jackie that under the rug in the dining room was a trapdoor to a crawl space where Grandma Garcia had kept bootlegged liquor.

Jackie related an experience she had with a spirit after owning the inn for about three months:

> I was running late. It was about 2:00 or 2:30 in the afternoon, and check-in was at three o'clock. I'm running around and see a gentleman wearing a long trench coat standing at the big double sink in the bathroom. He had long gray hair, very unkempt and dusty. I remember thinking, "Honestly, if you didn't lock the door, people would come in and they would wander around and use the bathrooms." So I thought someone had left the door unlocked. I stopped, and he went all the way in and around the corner. It was a big bathroom. I was busy trying to get ready for check-in. So I shut the vacuum off and knock on the big enclosure: "Sir, sir, we don't have public restrooms." I got around to where the commode was, and he wasn't there. There was a big window that went out to the second-floor balcony, so I opened it and looked out, and he was not out there. So I'm standing there for a moment, and then remember that underneath the double sink is a lot of storage so I look for him in there. He's not there. I look in the tub shower, and I am thinking, "Where in the hell did he go?" I finally call Allen [Jackie's husband and our esteemed Jerome police chief] and I tell him about this guy, and that I saw him walking around the corner. Allen asked for a description. Then he says, "Well, you know you are working a lot of hours." I told him I was not hallucinating in the middle of the afternoon! I could have brushed the dust off the intruder he was so real. He was wearing a canvas or leather duster that was really creepy. So I thought about it and didn't tell anyone but Allen. I wasn't scared. I wanted to make sense of it and be rational. I didn't think he could have jumped off the second-floor balcony. There was literally not enough time, and nowhere he could have gone!

Shortly after that experience, Jackie had another curious encounter. The big collection of room keys she always kept pinned to her jeans disappeared one day. Jackie had gone to the office and set them on her registration book, in which she tracks reservations and room availability. She went to the kitchen to do something, and when she came back, the keys were gone. She thought,

"What the hell?" Jackie looked everywhere, even places she knew she hadn't gone. It was a heavy mass of keys, including all her master keys. She broke down in tears and wondered, "Am I losing my mind?" She went back into the office, and to her surprise, the keys were back on top of her registration book! She called her mother and told her what happened, reassured that her mother would also believe she was losing her mind. Her mother replied, "Oh honey, I wouldn't share these stories with anyone. Don't tell anybody." About a year later, her mother advised Jackie to hire an exorcist.

Jackie's next spirit experience happened with a female guest after about a year and a half of owning the inn. The guest was an accountant from back east. She and her friend were up in the Verde View room, one of the rooms with the most activity. The accountant wasn't there for more than five minutes when she came down and said to Jackie, "You have seen him, haven't you? Well, he is up there. He is not trying to scare you. If it really bothers you, you can go into every room in here and ask him to leave you alone. You will never have another experience." Jackie thought the guest was whacked.

The guest continued, "I don't want to scare you, but I know some things about you and your husband." Jackie thought to herself, "There is nothing she could possibly know—she just got to town!" The guest said, "If your husband doesn't wear his back brace, he'll have to have significant back surgery." Three days before, Allen had gotten a molded back brace he was supposed to wear twenty-three hours a day. He had made it a half hour and said he couldn't do it. *This* caught Jackie's attention.

Then the guest said, "I have a grandmother here who would like to communicate with you." Jackie had lived with her grandmother until she was about five years old. "She wants to know if Jackie is eating meat yet or is she still living on cottage cheese and milk?" Jackie's father was an avid hunter and hunted everything: raccoon, beaver, deer, whatever was in season. Jackie wouldn't eat any of it. She would come home to a stinky roast with a trochanter hanging out, and her mom would say it came from the meat market. Jackie knew they didn't cut meat like that. The guest went on. She asked Jackie if she had two sons; she did. The guest relayed that her grandmother would like her to stop helping her eldest son financially, that she was not doing him any favors at all.

"I've stopped helping him," Jackie claimed. The guest said, "No." Jackie had lied, and the guest knew it. This also got Jackie's attention because she had just sent her son in Michigan $800 "because of another tragic whatever." The guest confirmed that there were spirits in the inn. "There is a spirit of a woman here named Grandma Garcia. She doesn't want any smoking or flames of any kind in or near the building because it had caught fire one time." The spirit of Grandma Garcia shows up on the porch shaking her finger when someone lights a cigarette.

Over the years, other people would see the cowboy in the leather duster. One of Allen's police officers said that she had seen the cowboy on the porch on the second floor, all dressed up.

Another time, a guest staying in the same room said she was sleeping when her husband got up to use the bathroom. The rooms are really small, so the bathroom door is right at the foot of the bed. When he came back, he kept moving about and woke up his wife. She sat up to ask him to stop when she realized it wasn't her husband at all. At the foot of the bed was the spirit of a man. She screamed and he disappeared.

Jackie said they wouldn't talk about the spirits with their guests, knowing they scared some people. The most common experience guests have had is hearing people walking around and slamming doors, likely getting ready for work at the mine. But the same description of the cowboy was reported time and time again.

Who *was* this mystery cowboy at the inn? Jackie said that years ago, someone she knew researched the story and the name Jake Stark had come up. Legend has it that he had been killed. One guest at the inn who saw Jake Stark, the cowboy in the night, said they had a nonverbal exchange—Jake conveyed to the guest that Cecil Thompson had murdered him. The Thompson family were kicked out of Jerome because they were hell-raisers.

Another guest at the inn told Jackie that he woke up in the middle of the night because he said there was movement at the foot of his bed—it was the spirit of a man. The guest hollered, and the spirit stood up! He was wearing a duster and went straight through the wall.

Ghost City Inn keeps journals in each guestroom so people can share their experiences if they so choose. "A lot of people write down what they saw because they are afraid to share it otherwise," said Jackie, "because people would think they were nuts." The experiences would happen in streaks, and guests would talk about it at breakfast. Or if they weren't quite so disclosing, they would call Jackie after checking out and ask, "Has anyone ever…?"

Another time, Jackie had a group book all the rooms at the inn, and only a few of the guests spoke English. They all spoke Spanish, and two sisters stayed in one of the rooms together. The next day, one of the sisters reported that in the middle of the night she was awakened by Grandma Garcia. "She shook me and chewed my ass out in Spanish!" Grandma Garcia also told her that if she didn't stop what she was doing, she was going to die. Come to find out this woman in her thirties was doing heavy drugs that none of the family knew about.

One time, a group of people from California came to stay. They spoke Spanish, and only a few of them spoke good English. One woman, who was Italian, had lived in the Gulch as a teenager. Jerome was segregated then: Mexicantown, Chinatown and so on. The elderly Italian woman was sitting in the dining room, and another woman was translating for her. Jackie was in the kitchen. "She had gotten pregnant by a Mexican [man] when she was fourteen years old," said Jackie. "In their culture, back then, that was worse than if you had murdered someone. She was sent to California to live with relatives, who made her give the baby away. This was her first trip back to Jerome…all she did was cry because everywhere she looked brought back the memories."

Jackie was raised Catholic, so anything having to do with ghosts was taboo, which is why her mother suggested she get an exorcist for the Ghost City Inn. "I told her whatever it was, it wasn't sinister," said Jackie. "It was nothing that made me feel like evil was going on. I never felt afraid." After Jackie had gone from room to room, asking the spirits to leave her alone, as the psychic accountant guest had suggested, she never had another thing happen.

Before making her request to the spirits, Jackie would go to the kitchen and think that somebody was with her, but nobody would be there. She would hear people upstairs after everyone had checked out, go investigate and find the place empty.

Nervous guests would tell Jackie they were scared. She would pass on the advice given to her: "Say to them, out loud, you don't want any experiences, that it freaks you out." And they would be left alone.

Nicole, a former Jerome police officer, had a spirit experience near the inn. She was attending the police academy in Prescott at the time, and one evening, she was heading home over Mingus Mountain, through Jerome to Clarkdale. It was dusk. As she made the hairpin turn just in front of the Ghost City Inn, she saw a figure standing in the middle of the road. Nicole knew that the figure was not really there because it was transparent. She drove right into it and slammed on her brakes. Then she thought, "What just happened?"

The male spirit was about six feet, four inches tall, gaunt, with prominent cheekbones, and he was wearing a duster-type coat and some kind of hat. He was looking straight at her. She remembered thinking, "That transparent dude has the most prominent cheekbones!" She said she would have taken him for a miner. She continued driving down the hill, and by the time she got to Clarkdale, her whole electrical system was fried—alternator, battery, she lost everything on the way down! She had to coast into the gas station at the bottom of the hill. She made it, but then thought, "That spirit just cost me hundreds of dollars!"

Nicole shared another story she had heard from a guest who stayed in the Cleopatra room at the inn. "She was the coolest lady....She said she was just sitting there and started feeling weird. Then whack! She was slapped across the face! She said you could see a full-on handprint. Her boyfriend was like, 'What the hell!?'"

A short distance from the inn, farther down 89A toward Cottonwood, across from the Methodist church, is the ruin of one of Jerome's grade schools. Bill, an esteemed Jerome resident and former fireman, has seen the apparition of a man in a fedora carrying a briefcase run across the sidewalk toward the school on three different occasions.

WALKING EACH OTHER HOME

HOGBACK CEMETERY AND
JEROME VALLEY CEMETERY

Jerome's old cemetery lies at the bottom of Hogback Ridge, down the hill from the main part of town. The cemetery is considered abandoned, with many broken headstones and unmarked grave sites.

There are reportedly more than four hundred graves at the Hogback Cemetery. However, fewer than forty headstones exist. I was told that about twenty-five years ago, a movie was made here for which several headstones were relocated, and the road from North Drive through the graveyard traverses over old grave sites. A resident of a house that no longer stands rerouted the road himself because he didn't want it so close to his home. Locals report that you can hear the different hollow sounds when you walk over a grave site as compared to solid earth.

The grave markers that are still legible show dates from 1897 to 1942 and are in several different languages. As noted in the well-researched book *Jerome, Arizona Cemeteries: Gone but Not Forgotten*, "There is evidence of many cultural groups within the cemeteries. Entombed...are immigrants from England, Ireland, Croatia, Spain, Mexico, China, Italy, France, Poland, Canada, Austria, Sweden, Yugoslavia, and Germany."

Here's a brief sampling (not a complete list by any means) of mining accidents that caused some of these deaths and potential spirits:

- severe burns received from the smelter
- fall down a mine shaft
- inhalation of carbonic acid

Hogback Cemetery, one mile from downtown, is full to capacity. Many graves were originally surrounded in wrought iron. *Copyright Michael Thompson.*

- mining accident where both legs were amputated causing immediate death
- skull fractured by falling rocks
- inhalation of toxic vapors/gases in the mine
- surgical shock due to amputation of fractured femur
- burns received over 75 percent of the body
- accidentally crushed under logs in the mine
- accidental electrocution
- run over by a train
- powder explosion
- run over by a slag motor
- fractures of the pelvis and laceration of the perineal tissues
- suffocated in a mine cave-in

And here's a short, incomplete list of murders that can account for some of the spirits:

- gunshot wounds
- blow to the head
- throat cut
- gunshot to the head

- gunshot to the right side of the chest
- stabbed with knife
- shoot out
- struck on the head by a bottle
- hit on the head with a shovel

Illnesses were also the cause of many deaths. Here's an abbreviated list:

- bronchopneumonia
- pulmonary tuberculosis
- acute leukemia
- influenza
- chronic atrophic hepatic cirrhosis
- myocarditis and dropsy
- smallpox
- organic heart disease and nephritis
- acute enteritis
- tubercular meningitis
- septicemia
- chronic gastroenteritis
- "summer complaint," which is acute diarrhea
- syphilis
- asthma

The Jerome Valley Cemetery is located down the mountain outside Clarkdale. It was established when the town experienced a severe outbreak of influenza. This cemetery holds a reported seven hundred graves.

If you add up the approximate number of graves in each Jerome cemetery, it only amounts to 1,100 graves, not even close to the number of deaths that occurred in Jerome. We know that the last hospital, now the Grand Hotel, recorded more than 9,000 deaths during its brief time as a hospital. Where are the rest of the bodies? What happened to them?

It has been said that during the time of the 1918 influenza, so many corpses piled up that they began burning them in the smelter to dispose of the overwhelming number and keep the outbreak from getting worse.

One resident with deep family history in Jerome, and someone who has done considerable research himself, speculated that many bodies wound up in the slag pots, which is one reason why hauntings occur all over town. In those early days, there were no safety measures in place, so it is possible that if someone died, the

The town of Jerome is in the background. It's a beautiful location to rest in peace—but do they? *Copyright Michael Thompson.*

body would be thrown into the slag pot, crushed up and made into aggregate for the concrete used to construct the town buildings and sidewalks. With so many deaths caused by mining explosions and burnings, it is easy to imagine that some of these bodies would be disposed of in this surreptitious way. If this is so, and remnants of the deceased are indeed in the buildings and streets, it's no wonder Jerome is the mother lode of spirits and restless souls.

Another historical point to think about is how rough and isolated Jerome was at the turn of the century, perched about one mile high on Cleopatra Hill. At one point, Clark closed the mines when the workers were striking for a twenty-five-cent-per-day raise. People starved to death. They were trapped on the mountain with no public transportation. There was no place for them to go unless they rode a horse or walked.

One can only imagine the Depression years in Jerome, with no relief or public assistance. During the worst of it, from 1933 to 1935, some families would give their children to their neighbors in the hopes they wouldn't starve to death.

Prohibition in Arizona lasted from 1915 to 1933—five years before it hit the rest of the country. When I asked Roberto how it affected Jerome, he chuckled and said, "Prohibition never really hit Jerome!" If there was ever an isolated, mining camp that needed booze, Jerome was it. Franklin D. Roosevelt said it well when he ended Prohibition in 1933: "What America needs now is a drink."

BLUE MOON HOUSE

Another cherished and longtime Jerome resident, Leigh, who just passed this year, shared this account with me about buying her "Blue Moon" house next to the Hogback Cemetery:

> *I saw this little house for sale close to thirty-eight years ago. I was going around the corner and saw them putting the "For Sale" sign on this house next to the cemetery. The house overlooked the cemetery.*
>
> *I called the agent and I saw the house. As I walked through the furnished house, the agent told me that the woman, named Marcelina, had lived in this house for close to sixty years. Her husband had been killed working for the mining company. He and another fellow were up in the flume, and there was a flashflood, and it washed them all the way to Clarkdale. The mining company then gave her this house, and she loved it. This mining company used to take care of their own. As I walked around the house, I could feel the*

*presence of this small round, short, old Mexican woman following me....
The house went in a circle with a bathroom in the middle and an addition
on the other side, which was Marcelina's favorite room. We sat down, and I
asked the real estate lady how I might buy this house? She said that I needed to
have earnest money. She had me sit in Marcelina's favorite chair. Marcelina's
glasses were on the coffee table with a magazine. Her nephew had come in
and decided that she needed to be in a nursing home, and he took her there
physically, against her will. He got her up and put her in a car, and she died
two weeks later in the nursing home, so unhappy being pulled out of her home.
There was holy water, all kinds of her belongings still in the house. When we
redid the house, we put all those things in the wall.*

*I could feel the presence of Marcelina's spirit encouraging me to buy
the house. Lilly was the realtor, and she said, "You have to have earnest
money," and I asked what that was. I was young and had never bought a
house before. The realtor told me I needed five hundred dollars. Fortunately,
I had a girlfriend with me who said that she had cash in her underwear
drawer and offered to go home and get it. I put the money on the house and
then found nobody wanted to insure or finance it because it was Jerome all
those years ago. The reason I named the house Blue Moon is that I signed
the escrow papers on a blue moon.*

*We finally got it all put together, but I noticed that if I didn't have the
chair in the back room, in the corner where Marcelina liked to sit and drink
her coffee, or read or whatever she did, that things would move around. I
use that back room as a studio. The water heater, washing machine and
the dryer were all in that room until we moved them downstairs. However,
if she didn't have the chair there, then things would move around the house
that I couldn't find. I mean, I go through that anyway—I don't need a
spirit messing with my house!*

*So, years and years later, I rented it out after I married Richard and I
moved out of the house, and I would tell people that they needed to leave the
chair there. If they moved it, they would call me complaining and tell me
that somebody had been in the house. Marcelina's spirit was never violent.
However, she would get pushy if you didn't leave her chair where it was.*

*Then I did a vacation rental, and I had many, many guests who for six
or eight years would stay at the house for a weekend and they just loved it.*

*Guests would mention that they felt someone kissing them on the cheek
in bed....I thought that she had left when we ripped apart the house and
put in a basement and foundation. There had been no original foundation.
However, she came back.*

My mother had gotten a beautiful print in Paris years ago that I inherited, and it looked sort of like a ghost lady looking through wet pane glass windows. One day I came in to change the beds, and somebody had put a towel over that painting because it creeped them out. Somebody even got so freaked out that they had to leave, so I took all the information about the spirit off the vacation rental website. Some people thought it was not an attraction. Some thought it was cool, and others were freaked out!

A remarkable artifact was found in the area of the Blue Moon house and the Tamale Ladies' house, which are across the street from each other. North Drive merges into Dundee, and at the end of Dundee was the original town dump. Homeowners on North and Dundee would find trash material that had been dumped years ago. Bill and his family lived not far from the Tamale Ladies, and one day he happened to notice his grandchildren playing a cowboy game with a gun. Then he realized that it *wasn't* a pretend gun and wondered where they'd found it. Shockingly, it was an old flintlock handgun that the children had found in the dirt on his property. It's likely that the old

Discovered on property by owners' grandchildren when they were playing in the yard. It was located near the cemetery and the old town dump. *Photo by Midge Steuber.*

gun ended up there because the town had burned down so many times in the mining years that the ruins would be scooped up and hauled off to the dump.

Whose gun was this? If it could only talk…

TAMALE LADIES

Aurelia Gonzalez, who arrived in Jerome in 1926, and Santos Contreras, who came in 1944, were sisters. They lived in a house at the top of North Drive and would make tamales and bring them uptown to sell, hence their nickname. They were a well-loved institution in Jerome, and we would be remiss not to mention them. Roberto reported, with a twinkle in his eye and compassion in his heart, that Aurelia was amazing. "Her courtesy, genteelness and her manners, which she used to minimize and say, 'I am just a little girl from the rancho…' She was that, but she was also one of the nicest persons you could ever meet."

Roberto wrote a true story about them called "The Millionaire and the Tamale Lady" in *Rich Town Poor Town*. Aurelia's husband, José, was a favorite of Rawhide Jimmy Douglas. José contracted tuberculosis, was put in the dead room in the hospital and then released. He committed suicide when he got out because he could not work in the mine any longer and support his family. He shot himself on the road, right in front of the Tamale Ladies' house. That was 1949. Aurelia gave Roberto the .32-caliber pistol José had used. From that day forward, Aurelia was a widow with no Social Security and no money saved up.

People had already started leaving Jerome when José committed suicide in 1949. The demand for copper plummeted, and copper prices fell at the end of World War II in 1945, when copper wasn't needed for shells and bullets. The town was dying.

Aurelia and Santos needed a way to survive, so they began making and selling tamales. The sisters would walk from the cemetery all the way up town each day, carrying a bucket of tamales and selling them along the way. Jerry Vojnic, owner of Paul and Jerry's Saloon, told them that for the price they were asking they were not going to make any money, so he told them what to charge and they survived.

Jane used to see the Tamale Ladies walking up to the post office every day, even though she is sure they were in their nineties by then. When Jane would go riding her horses and pass by the Tamale Ladies' house, she would always see them sitting on their porch, and they would share a brief greeting. One of the ladies told Jane that her key to longevity was a beer and a cigarette every day.

CONCLUSION

We are convinced that the spirits are still here in Jerome. The evidence is overwhelming. Spirits sometimes linger when their lives are suddenly cut short.

Most people don't believe in ghosts until something happens to them. We think many spirits here are good, but there are parts of town where evil lurks, places where untold debauchery took place. Mining and smelting were, and are, dangerous jobs, and the mining corporations could be both generous and cruel. Horrible accidents transpired here.

Jerome was practically abandoned once the mines closed in the early 1950s. The hippies arrived in the late 1960s and early '70s. Conditions in town were perfect for young, energetic, creative people. Because of their appearance, the locals who still lived in town were afraid of the hippies. It took them about ten years to realize that they were just a bunch of educated, creative kids. The hippies had a can-do attitude and began to fix the infrastructure and the business district. They wanted an artists' town, and in time they built it.

What you see today is still that town. Jerome provides an enjoyable experience created by its rich history and creative artists. In our community, neighbors look after one another. It's another reason Jerome is so special.

The spirits of the mining days linger, as the testimonies in this book attest. We hope you enjoyed them.

Current photograph of Jerome. You can see John McMillian's trees in the foreground covered in snow. *Copyright Ron Chilston.*

New State Motor Company building, next to the Sullivan Hotel, formerly Belgian Jennie's "Honky Tonk House of Light and Love." *Copyright Ron Chilston.*

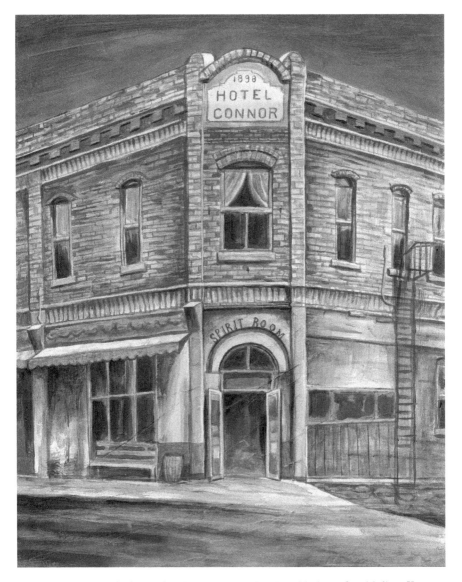

Artist rendering, oil: *The Connor Hotel*. You can almost feel the spirits here. *Copyright Jason Voss.*

When you walk in Jerome
You never walk alone
'Cause the ghosts dance all around you
All around you in Jerome
　　　　　—"Jerome," by the Barenaked Ladies

SELECTED BIBLIOGRAPHY

DeCamp, Rosemary. *Tigers in My Lap.* Parkville, MD: Midnight Marquee Press, 2009

Hicks, Peggy. *Are Ghosts Real? The Story of Belgian Jennie.* Jerome: Arizona Discoveries, 2016.

———. *The Ghosts of the Cuban Queen.* Jerome: Arizona Discoveries, 2014.

Rabago, Roberto. *Rich Town Poor Town: Ghosts of Copper's Past.* Jerome, AZ: Multicultural Educational Publishing Company, 2011.

Rees, Elizabeth, Joan Evans and Ann Rees. *Jerome, Arizona Cemeteries: Gone but Not Forgotten.* Sold at the Jerome Historical Society, n.d.

Steuber, Midge. *Jerome.* Charleston, SC: Arcadia Publishing Company, 2008.

Young, Herbert V. *Ghosts of Cleopatra Hill: Men and Legends of Old Jerome.* Jerome, AZ: Jerome Historical Society, 1964.

———. *They Came to Jerome: The Billion Dollar Copper Camp.* Jerome, AZ: Jerome Historical Society, 1972.

ABOUT THE AUTHORS

PATRICIA S. JACOBSON has lived in Jerome for almost forty years, or most of her life. Originally from Chicago, Pat started visiting Jerome in 1973 when a good friend moved to town. Pat was an art student at Arizona State University, about one hundred miles away. The ladies she knew in Jerome were getting horses. An equestrian herself, she would travel to Jerome to help with them. It was a magical time.

Pat's first experience with Jerome spirits—and one she'll never forget—was in the 1970s. She was following friends down a stairway in the Company Hill area when suddenly she felt a very large, meaty hand on her back shove her. But instead of tumbling down into her friends ahead of her, Pat flew over them and landed in the parking lot. She knew then that a ghost had pushed her.

Jerome was in its early stages of restoration at this time. Pat was able to explore the abandoned buildings on Main Street. She studied the history and curated historical art shows, including a Lew Davis retrospective. Davis was born in Jerome and painted the miners during the 1930s and '40s. His paintings are in many significant art collections.

Pat finally moved to Jerome in 1980 to become the director of the Verde Valley Art Association. She fell in love with Jerome and the local artists. Not only was the view spectacular, but the community was also wonderful. Pat bought a sweet little Mustang mare and began to ride the stagecoach roads and old railroad trails. She explored the underbelly of Jerome with several employees of the Phelps Dodge mining company and went way beyond the "No Trespassing" signs. Pat knows where all the train tunnels and the old change houses are, now completely off limits. She has seen wildcat mines in the middle of nowhere and rotting head frames over dangerous deep holes. She has ridden through the decaying empire built by William Clark.

Pat became a musician after leaving the art association, playing the fiddle and mandolin in Jerome and throughout Arizona with several bands for twenty-five years.

In 1988, Pat bought a house built in 1910, which she has been restoring ever since. Yes, she has had to deal with the spirits in the house; she thinks they have honored her request to leave, but not all paranormal investigators agree.

Pat became the first ghost-hunting guide in Jerome and worked for five years designing and conducting historical tours and paranormal investigations. She's led at least a thousand ghost tours and has turned up unexplained evidence on almost every tour! One never knows what lurks in the shadows.

MIDGE STEUBER's professional training is in psychology, although she has worked in a variety of fields. She's been a Good Humor ice cream truck driver, a Merrill Lynch stockbroker, a counselor for a rape crisis center and battered women's shelter, a healthcare provider for two nonprofit hospice companies, a real estate investor and more.

Midge is mostly your middle-aged woman lucky enough to find a community of kindred spirits. Jerome has been her haven for close to sixteen years. It is said in town that folks don't actually move here but are called here. This is how it has felt for Midge—it's been a very comfortable fit from the get-go.

The first four people she met when she arrived told her, "Jerome is not a town; Jerome is a family. Welcome home." Soothing words to her gypsy soul.

Jerome has cradled her, protected her and supported her through tough times, for which she is grateful. Jerome is her refuge and base camp.

During the process of writing this book and listening to credible people tell story after story of different hauntings in town, Midge can now say that she is a believer in ghosts. Their existence is something she can no longer deny.

Something is definitely going on in Jerome.

Favorite quote:
"In the end, just three things matter: How well we have lived, how well we have loved, and how well we have learned to let go." –Jack Kornfield

Visit us at
www.historypress.com

Printed in the USA
CPSIA information can be obtained
at www.ICGtesting.com
LVHW061523030324
773429LV00007B/32